The Tacit Dimension

The Tacit Dimension

Architecture Knowledge and Scientific Research

Edited by Lara Schrijver

Leuven University Press

This publication was made possible by funding from the Netherlands Organisation for Scientific Research (IGW, 2014–2016, project no. 236-57-001), from the European Union's Horizon 2020 research and innovation programme (Marie Skłodowska-Curie grant agreement no. 860413), and KU Leuven Fund for Fair Open Access.

Published in 2021 by Leuven University Press / Presses Universitaires de Louvain / Universitaire Pers Leuven. Minderbroedersstraat 4, B-3000 Leuven (Belgium).

© Selection and editorial matter: Lara Schrijver, 2021
© Individual chapters: the respective authors, 2021

This book is published under a Creative Commons Attribution Non-Commercial Non-Derivative 4.0 Licence. Further details about Creative Commons licences are available at http://creativecommons.org/licenses/ Attribution should include the following information: Lara Schrijver (ed.), *The Tacit Dimension: Architecture Knowledge and Scientific Research*. Leuven, Leuven University Press. (CC BY-NC-ND 4.0)

ISBN 978 94 6270 271 4 (Paperback)
ISBN 978 94 6166 380 1 (ePDF)
ISBN 978 94 6166 381 8 (ePUB)
https://doi.org/10.11116/9789461663801
D/2021/1869/12
NUR: 648

Layout & cover design: DOGMA
Cover illustration: 'Uber taxi driver in Shenzhen' 2015. Ink on paper 50×65 cm, Jan Rothuizen, from a series for the Shenzhen Bi-city Biennale of Urbanism/Architecture 2015.

Contents

Introduction: Tacit Knowledge, Architecture and its Underpinnings   7
Lara Schrijver

Performative Design Research: En-acting Knowledge in Teaching   23
Angelika Schnell

Teaching Architecture Full Scale   37
Mari Lending

Transformative Dialogues: On Material Knowing in Architecture   55
Eireen Schreurs

A Black Box? Architecture and its Epistemes   69
Tom Avermaete

Design Knowledges on the Move   83
Margitta Buchert

A Silent Master: Artistry and Craft in the Work of Peter Celsing   97
Christoph Grafe

Material Knowledge and Cultural Values   113
Lara Schrijver

About the Authors   125

Introduction: Tacit Knowledge, Architecture and its Underpinnings

Lara Schrijver

This book addresses the idea of 'tacit knowledge', posited over 50 years ago by Hungarian intellectual Michael Polanyi, as a perspective that helps the discipline of architecture to (re)connect its practices and theories, and contributes to a better understanding of the built environment as a phenomenon that both reflects and shapes cultures and contexts.[1] The very notion of tacit knowledge addresses the growing awareness that abilities and unstated habits and assumptions are equally formative for our intellectual understanding as the more formal, codified things we learn. This aspect is particularly prominent in another scholar's work that provided a foundation for Polanyi to expand upon. Just after World War II, Gilbert Ryle addressed the Aristotle Society with the suggestion that philosophy had neglected a fundamental problem by typically addressing explicit knowledge ('knowing that'), rather than the knowledge inherent in abilities ('knowing how').[2] In essence, Ryle suggests we 'know' far more than philosophy has been able to trace, as it has neglected particular skills as a knowledge base. Following on his heels, Polanyi states that 'we can know more than we can tell'. Both these philosophers thus draw attention to the limitations of scientific and philosophical approaches to knowledge when they fail to take into account the type of knowledge or learning that cannot be quantified or codified; both draw attention to context-dependency and the embodied aspects of knowledge and understanding.

Today, the interest in tacit aspects of knowledge is rising. As the awareness grows that rational thinking alone is insufficient to address the cultural modulations that also make up society, the interest in unstated assumptions and drives increases.[3] In architecture in particular, the entanglements between the built environment, cultural habits, and the impact on the natural environment are coming ever more clearly into focus, driving a need to understand the more hidden effects of architectural design and its cultures.[4] At the same time, this need for a broader and more in-depth understanding of the impact of architecture runs counter to two specific habits of architecture education in the twentieth century: it challenges the perception of the architect as visionary, a carry-over from modernism that remains present in many curricula; and it seeks to expand the rationalized understanding of architecture that grew in importance as architecture schools became further incorporated into university programmes, demanding more clearly delineated research projects. Moreover, in many architecture schools, the studio curricula are still strongly defined by the master-student relationship, which can strengthen the hidden biases of the discipline.

Within these limitations, however, the learning and practice of architecture provide rich ground for addressing tacit dimensions of knowing. As architecture itself often shows more than it tells, the history and theory of architecture provide a useful reflective lens to address these questions of different aspects of knowing. Architecture is by nature a discipline that makes use of both explicit and tacit knowledge, expressing its concepts and ideas through drawing and notational skills in order to realize a (projected) material reality. It is a practice informed by personal preferences, cultural context and a disciplinary *habitus*. As such, it brings together numerous aspects of the discourse on tacit knowledge. Unravelling some of its histories can provide additional insights into various dimensions of the tacit, such as skill-based knowledge, unstated cultural and disciplinary habits and the limits of codified knowledge. In essence, the work in this book also suggests that as a field, architecture already included ideas around tacit knowledge before it was identified as such. Conversely, a direct exploration of the dimensions of tacit knowledge can aid in increasing the understanding between codified knowledge, innovative research, and the domain of architectural practices, which is where our built environment is actually shaped, built on the underlying assumptions and state of the art.

This rising interest in what we might for now call 'alternative modes of knowing' (including notions such as precognitive thought, tacit knowledge and embodied reflection) illustrates a perhaps natural desire for a counterweight to the increasing and continuing rationalization that has been tangible since the rise of industrialization, and that has become increasingly widespread since the beginning of the twentieth century.[5] The various expressions of 'tacit knowing' presented in this book show the boundaries of what we can rationally understand and what we can codify.

Today, many disciplines are seeking a better understanding of tacit knowledge in order to gain insight into how people work and communicate – together and individually – how organizations work, and which unstated assumptions inform our perceptions and ideas. Current scientific work confirms the relevance of this interest in the tacit, in the sense that management studies have found it necessary to understand more than just the formal interactions between people, and that in social and political philosophy, some of the underlying assumptions have begun to come into focus as driving more than just emotions and sensibilities, thereby driving our thoughts and actions in manners that cannot be explained *only* from the perspective of rationality.[6] Indeed as some of the insights from the neurosciences and psychology begin to confirm our ideas that much 'thinking' is done *prior* to clear cognitive recognition of thought, some of the classic clichés, such as pictures being worth a thousand words, can gain in depth – if we are prepared to study the 'argument' being put forward.[7]

Building on this broader understanding of how we know things, this book suggests that architecture can shed light on both the disconnection between articulable, codified thought and the hidden assumptions that underpin them, as well as on their mutual influence. The hypothesis here is that – alongside other appraisals of the profession – there are particular aspects of the architectural profession that are closely aligned with what is written on tacit knowledge, and that the interaction between material, concrete objects, a complicated, social practice and its own disciplinary theories aids in identifying this field of relations (if not always in understanding it). To add to the complexities, the engagement with the object for an architect is typically at a remove; the drawings of a building are not its final aim, but a real building is – and as such the drawings and models that aim at its realization form a second filter of both codified knowledge and implicit assumptions that are part and parcel of the discipline.[8] At the same time, as architecture has become more defined by scientific research, it has also made important progress in more traditional areas of scientific inquiry, particularly when it pertains to structural engineering and quantifiable factors of building quality such as ventilation.

In engaging with this complexity, architects have regularly been confronted with the distinctions and discrepancies between what they can *tell* and what they can *know*, as well as what they can *show* in drawings and models. As such, tracing through the recent histories of architecture, from a historical and practice-based perspective, sheds some light on the interaction between thinking and doing, and on the assumptions that underpin the codified language of the architecture discipline.

Tacit knowledge: from cognitive thinking to embodied insight

Overall, this book seeks to trace back the foundations of thinking about tacit knowledge, and connect them to historical developments in architecture. In so doing, it provides a skill-based perspective on the experiential dichotomy of thinking and making – one that is intimately familiar to anyone who has learned to ride a bicycle or to drive, who has learned to play a musical instrument or to cook; the principles behind these activities can all be explained in great detail and at great length, but it is in the actual execution – and longstanding practice – that one begins to sense an *embodied knowledge* that guides these abilities. This is what Polanyi identifies as the 'intelligent effort' that is needed to bridge the gap between theoretical principles and the integrated performance of an activity. The moment the hand knows what to do before the brain can abstractly tell it is precisely what underpins the philosophical problem first identified by Ryle and subsequently explored in depth by Polanyi.

For Ryle, this consisted of 'knowing that' versus 'knowing how', and realizing that in philosophy, abilities had been treated purely as an *application* of conceptual knowledge. Once one knows what is true, one can apply this, demonstrating knowledge of principles in the activity. But this conception, to Ryle, neglects many dimensions of experience and neglects to account for how knowing can be actualized in the exercise of a skill.⁹ Does a baseball pitcher who throws a perfect curveball thereby demonstrate and apply a thorough knowledge of physics? Or is it rather a cumulative knowledge built up from the experience of having thrown thousands of pitches? And should we expect that a bright physicist will be able to excel at that perfect curveball? Likewise, when learning to cook, each aspect of the activity can be explained, but how does one build up the knowledge to know when something is cooked to perfection? Most experienced cooks will say they just 'know'. And largely, this will be based on sight, smell, touch, sound – sensory perceptions that have rarely factored into understanding how knowledge works, and dimensions that are central to the current discourse on architecture thinking.

For Polanyi, Ryle presented an interesting problem, but his division between skill/ability (knowing how) and intellectual understanding (knowing that) did not sufficiently address the issue of how to understand the cumulative nature of knowledge that builds up in activities. While some of this was hinted at in Ryle's first foray into the gap between doing and thinking, it was Polanyi who more thoroughly explored the process of learning and the different stages of knowledge acquisition within skills and abilities. In so doing, he makes a distinction between the integration of focal and subsidiary aspects of knowledge. His description of the process of acquiring different levels of expertise helps to understand how some elements can become invisible and, therefore, not part of a discourse on knowledge. For example, in the process of learning a physical skill – playing the piano or riding a bicycle, for example – it is first necessary to practice individual aspects. This includes such things as becoming accomplished at finding the right keys on the piano or at steering the bicycle while you pedal. This first stage means an individuated concentration on partial aspects. Each of these individual aspects may be a focal point in the early stages of knowledge and skill acquisition, but when a basic level of expertise has been achieved, automation allows for a new focus, on perfecting the performance.¹⁰ As the individual components of these skills are only apprehended in terms of the intended performance, they do not match our understanding of (explicit) knowledge. Instead, Polanyi's explanation reveals both the tacit aspects and the complementary operations of subsidiary and focal elements.¹¹

While the relevance of tacit knowledge may seem self-evident from the perspective of today – as recent economic theories have amply demonstrated the shortcomings of understanding human behaviour as primarily rational – it is easy to overlook the difficulty of incorporating new insights into academic discourse. Longstanding preconceptions are highly resistant to change, and our biases are coded into many aspects of culture and thinking, thereby being continually reinforced in habits, practices and even 'objective' scientific inquiry.[12] As such, we should be even more aware of how strong the bias against new ideas has often been – while the work of Donna Haraway now seems central in a time when the lines of gendered thinking are shifting, her ideas on cyborgs and post-feminism seemed radical for many years after the first publication of the 'Cyborg Manifesto'.[13] As such, it is also important to realize how much the research presented here owes to the diverse ecosystem of thinking and criticism of the post-war era, particularly with the situated and relational understanding of knowledge that came out of feminism and science and technology studies.[14]

Architecture's parallels

Three periods in architecture history hold particular interest in terms of the insights derived through abilities and habits versus those of cognitive and codified knowledge. These examples each show the entanglement of practice and theory, of underlying cultural transformation and new material forms. In the nineteenth century, the remarkable technological innovations that initiated machine production and the broader systematization of knowledge contributed to a reconfiguring of both the landscape of knowledge and of material production. In the early twentieth century, the Bauhaus brought together the strands of industrial production, artistic spirit and the principles of the workshop into its own particular style of schooling, which was to fan out over the United States following the closure of the school. In the 1970s, a different situation, particularly in America, gave reason for many architecture schools to expand their programmes to include a more substantial programme in history and other fields of study, as these professional schools increased the scholarly elements of their curricula, falling more in line with traditional university programmes while maintaining their studio-oriented focus.[15] In this period, Donald Schön's ideas on the 'reflective practitioner' helped to address the design process as an area that also merited further study to adequately explain the many facets of thinking and doing.[16]

While Ryle presented something new with his address on knowing how and knowing that, the domains of art and architecture had already shown the divisions between the labour of the mind and the labour of the hand earlier in history. Notably in architecture, the notion of *disegno* in the Renaissance signified the separation between the conception of design and the craft of building.[17] In the Enlightenment, new institutional arrangements transformed how knowledge was gathered, structured and disseminated; eighteenth-century France provides a good example of how the abstract scientific knowledge represented by the *Académie des Sciences* became increasingly preferred to the skill-based knowledge of the *Société des Arts et Métiers*.[18] While many of the *métiers* provided crucial insights to the *Académie des Sciences*, it was the abstract intellectual exercise of philosophical and scientific thought that became hierarchically more valuable than the knowledge derived from practice and skill. This continues to be visible throughout the twentieth century, and clearly underpins the later dismissal of practice-based professions as less rigorous or scientifically valid.[19]

Today, however, this continuing trajectory of rationalization, founded on the Enlightenment and grounded in the principles of natural science, is reaching a turning point. Recent insights from neuroscience and cognitive science have encouraged increasing attention on the embodiment of knowledge, providing scientific evidence for Polanyi's hypothesis that there is more to knowing than what we can codify or make explicit.[20] This extends to studies in the social sciences, which demonstrate how traditions, habits and customs are passed on and cemented within organizations, and to experimental sciences, which sometimes observe unexpected effects and make use of the space between idea and execution in order to find new insights.[21]

From profession to discipline: integrating knowledge in architecture

In architecture, the longstanding gap between the conception of a building and its realization has further solidified in the growing distinction between designer and craftsman. This separation has allowed the artist's conception to gain primacy over the craftsman's knowledge and development of building practices, which in the modern era have often been seen as 'mere building'. While this was extended and cemented by the desire to become a university-based discipline, it is here that in the 1970s and 1980s some of the difficulties began to arise. In 1974, Nathan Glazer dismissed many new disciplines as 'minor professions' founded on skills rather than science, a statement that might have been more readily countered if the earlier philosophical explorations of the gap between skill and knowledge had been better incorporated in the studies.[22] At the same time, Donald Schön introduced the notion of the reflective practitioner, suggesting that studio approaches added a new dimension to established insights on problem-solving. Schön described the studious manner in which design problems and possible solutions were continually reworked in relation to multiple constraints and intentions, and concluded that in the drawing process, a skill-based knowledge emerged, which he identified as a reflective practice.[23] These two thinkers show the tensions that arose as numerous fields largely based in practice became part of the university and even today continue to inform debates on research methods.

During this latest period of recalibrating scientific methods, the field of industrial design, in particular, provided influential ideas. Bryan Lawson and Nigel Cross both argued that 'designerly ways of knowing' were a separate category of knowledge that was accompanied by a different approach to problem-solving (or even 'problem-finding', according to Lawson).[24] In short, Cross argued that the knowledge construction of the natural sciences is aimed at *understanding* the world around us and founded on *analysis* of existing phenomena; the humanities are oriented on *insight* into human motivation and founded on *reflection*; and the design fields are focused on *transforming* the world, based on the *creation* of new structures, objects and things. In experiments, Lawson showed that designers approached problem-solving in a synthetic manner, seeking out series of possible solutions, while natural scientists analysed the problem. In these works, they provided a way of speaking about the inductive and intuitive processes of design, and many scholars were to follow, expanding the resources and vocabulary for discussing other approaches to knowledge.[25]

Thinking forward: tacit practices and entangled knowledge

This book provides a synthesis of research and discussions held between 2013 and 2018, for which a start-up network brought together a number of European researchers addressing a similar intuition that there is more to say about the hidden underpinnings of architecture.[26] Each author has provided a short essay on a salient feature of tacit knowledge, which unfolds a specific aspect of the material, skill-based and design-oriented knowledge present in architecture.

Exploring elements of the learning process embedded in studio work, Angelika Schnell addresses performativity and its role in acquiring embodied knowledge. Here, the teaching process of the studio becomes a site of *enacting* knowledge, thereby linking implicit and explicit aspects of knowledge. By re-enacting a particular studio programme, aspects of understanding that cannot be disclosed in the space of a text become apparent; they become embodied through the process of learning-by-doing. Even as architecture training is becoming increasingly academic, the studio is a site of knowledge production that resists more traditional structures of academic teaching yet provides a common knowledge base founded on intersubjective judgements.

Mari Lending turns her eye to the materials used in teaching; she shows how plaster casts of existing built elements have been used in architectural education and exhibitions to directly activate the mimetic knowledge of historical precedent. Exploring the migration and dissemination of knowledge that becomes possible with these casts, she addresses how knowledge becomes present and visible in these material manifestations. Here, the process of assembling and curating the architectural object manifests the tacit knowledge of cultural histories and narratives. As materializations of abstract ideas, the in-depth studies of the aggregate, construction work and drawings express the value of experiential teaching in architecture, from the *École des Beaux-Arts* in Paris to the here and now.

This material perspective is further developed by Eireen Schreurs, who shows the impact of an embodied and reflective understanding of materials on developments in architecture. Examining Labrouste's explorations of iron as a construction material in the *Bibliothèque Nationale*, her essay studies the development of design thinking through the lens of material knowledge. It examines the presence and trajectory of materials in the design and building process, and their often implicit role in shaping architecture. As the discourse on material culture spreads rapidly throughout the humanities, specific cases in architecture such as these provide solid ground for reflecting on the presence and role of materials in constructing and embodying ideas.

Taking on the structure of ideas within the discipline, Tom Avermaete addresses the underlying assumptions that become visible within the design process, which has often been seen as a 'black box'. Avermaete seeks to relate accepted academic methodologies to approaches from design. Some scholars provide research perspectives that try to come closer to the designer, while others focus on material culture as an aid to understand the tacit dimension of design. This essay addresses a series of epistemes that allow for a design-based attitude to enrich the perspective of theory and history. The various epistemes presented by Avermaete provide a foundation for examining tacit knowledge at work in the field.

Margitta Buchert examines the roles of empathy, embodiment and reflexivity in design, revealing the fundamentally embodied nature of thinking and designing. Empathy has been underestimated both in architectural discourse and in the training of the architect. The essay differentiates two modes of empathy: one as constructed, disciplined experience and one as the open-minded observation of sensory issues of the building and the environment. These modes of experience highlight the sensitivities underpinning tacit knowledge and its interplay with explicit knowledge. Examining the findings of various disciplines through selected examples, Buchert brings to the foreground the entanglement of empathy and reflexivity, as well as modes of cognition at the intersection of tacit and explicit forms of knowledge in architectural design.

To show how tacit knowledge and contextual elements reside in the architect's craftsmanship, Christoph Grafe provides a close reading of Peter Celsing's work. Focusing on the materialization of contextual conditions, Grafe suggests that architecture embodies the particularities of its own context while being situated within a broader global discourse of aesthetics, habits and conventions. This essay addresses how practice is embedded in a particular context yet has underlying similarities with different contexts. Departing from the work of Peter Celsing, Grafe studies the global horizon of locally anchored architectural cultures, showing how the post-war moderns allow a local logic to attach and relate to international cultures.

Lara Schrijver addresses the cultural and contextual values that are materialized in works of architecture, exploring what object-oriented philosophies may hold for architecture thinking. Addressing the weakly defined relation between ethical positions and their corresponding aesthetic materialization, this essay shows how the ethical domain becomes explicitly articulated in form. Historically, many (early) modern writings have conflated moral and aesthetic concerns; is a productive relationship between aesthetics and values still conceivable? Schrijver explores normative positions from the implicit preferencing of craft to the ideological prioritizing of space to show where ethical positions are both clearly defined as ideas and loosely delineated to provide allowances in their realization.

These essays are presented in an expanding influence, from architectural education, its role in the public domain and the role of materials in the design process (Schnell, Lending, Schreurs), to the conceptual structures at play and the experience of implicit knowledge (Avermaete, Buchert), to an example of craft and the cultural context within which this knowledge arises (Grafe, Schrijver). In so doing, this book gathers a number of perspectives that explore the tacit dimensions of knowledge-in-making, the knowing of things, and the values that underpin embodied knowing, positioning these in terms of their relationship to the world at large. It provides a first step in thinking the tacit forward: gathering current insights in order to bring the longstanding presence of tacit knowledge in architecture into articulate focus – through words, and drawings, and diagrams and buildings.

The newly initiated research network TACK engages directly with this pressing need for an in-depth examination of tacit knowledge.[27] It aims to understand more qualitatively the underpinnings of architectural design, which is trained through repetition and reworking, until the sensory perspectives and embodied knowledge are a nearly invisible understanding *prior* to thinking through each step. While not all tacit knowledge should necessarily be made explicit, having an awareness of these hidden underpinning may aid in showing what disciplinary and skill-based knowledge continues to be valid, while perhaps other aspects may be elucidated and experimented upon. In fact, if we can shed the mysticism and romanticism that at times envelop the 'mysteries' of practice, we may indeed identify tools and methods that address contemporary challenges in a manner more sensitized to the multiple needs of the environment. As global infrastructure and institutions become increasingly entangled and the digital technologies we have developed spread a hidden set of values and ideas within the very infrastructures we communicate through, the impact of tacit knowledge and hidden assumptions is becoming more visible. The built environment shows a vast history of cultural contexts and assumptions materialized into an environment appraised in distraction, and thereby provides a specific and observable material precedent for the ephemeral and less tangible designs now infiltrating and thus shaping daily life. Delineating future lines of inquiry along the lines of theoretical understanding ('approaching tacit knowledge'), practice-based insight ('probing tacit knowledge') and entangled knowledge ('situating tacit knowledge'), the research network will explore these material and tangible constructions in the coming years.

Notes

1   See in particular Michael Polanyi, *The Tacit Dimension* (Chicago: University of Chicago Press, 1966) and the earlier essay 'Tacit Knowing: Its Bearing on Some Problems of Philosophy', *Reviews of Modern Physics* 34:4 (1962), 601–616.

2   Gilbert Ryle, 'Knowing How and Knowing That: The Presidential Address', *Proceedings of the Aristotelian Society* 46 (1946), 1–16.

3   For example, Daniel Kahneman is widely known for his research that challenges the idea of rationality as the basis for human decision-making. See Daniel Kahneman, Paul Slovic and Amos Tversky, *Judgment Under Uncertainty: Heuristics and Biases* (New York: Cambridge University Press, 1982).

4   An early exploration of these ideas in architecture is to be found in Deborah Hauptmann and Warren Neidich, (eds.), *Cognitive Architecture. From Biopolitics to Noopolitics. Architecture & Mind in the Age of Communication and Information* (Rotterdam: nai-010publishers, 2010).

5   As will be discussed below, these are various ideas that have gained traction in recent years; alongside Polanyi, see, for example, Francesco J. Varela et al., *The Embodied Mind: Cognitive Science and Human Experience*, revised edition (Cambridge, MA: MIT Press, 2017 [orig. 1991]); and Alva Noë, *Out of Our Heads: Why You Are Not Your Brain, and Other Lessons from the Biology of Consciousness* (New York: Farrar, Strauss and Giroux, 2009).

6   Notable authors that address underlying intuitions as both formative and informative are Daniel Kahneman, Stephen Turner and Alva Noë.

7   Alva Noë, *Out of Our Heads: Why You Are Not Your Brain, and Other Lessons from the Biology of Consciousness* (New York: Farrar, Strauss and Giroux, 2009).

8   Robin Evans, *Translations from Drawing to Building and Other Essays* (Cambridge, MA: MIT Press, 1996); Stan Allen, *Practice: Architecture, Technique and Representation* (Amsterdam: G+B Arts International, 2000).

9   Ryle, 'Knowing How and Knowing That', 10–11.

10 Michael Polanyi, *The Tacit Dimension* (Chicago: University of Chicago Press, 1966).

11 The complementary operations of subsidiary-focal integration become apparent in Polanyi's description of the type of knowledge demonstrated by a doctor's diagnostic skills, which include assessing a constellation of symptoms, not all of which will be easily situated within a codified, step-by-step analysis. Polanyi 'Tacit Knowing', 602–604.

12 Caroline Criado Perez, *Invisible Women: Data Bias in a World Designed for Men* (New York: Harry N. Abrams, 2019); Stefan Buijsman, *AI: Alsmaar Intelligenter* (Amsterdam: De Bezige Bij, 2020).

13 Donna Haraway, 'A Manifesto for Cyborgs: Science, Technology, and Socialist Feminism in the 1980s', *Socialist Review* 80 (1985), 65–107. Another influential work in this area is N. Katharine Hayles, *How We Became Posthuman: Virtual Bodies in Cybernetics, Literature and Informatics* (Chicago: University of Chicago Press, 1999).

14 For two prominent voices in this discourse, see Donna Haraway, 'Situated Knowledges: The Science Question in Feminism and the Privilege of Partial Perspective', *Feminist Studies* 14:3 (1988), 575–599; and Isabelle Stengers, 'Introductory Notes on an Ecology of Practices', *Cultural Studies Review* 11:1 (2005), 183–196.

15 Gwendolyn Wright, 'History for Architects', in: Gwendolyn Wright and Janet Parks (eds.), *The History of History in American Schools of Architecture 1865–1975* (New York: Temple Buell and Princeton Architectural Press, 1990); Alina A. Payne, 'Architectural History and the History of Art: A Suspended Dialogue', *Journal of the Society of Architectural Historians* 58:3 (1999), 292–299.

16 Donald A. Schon, *The Reflective Practitioner: How Professionals Think In Action* (New York: Basic Books, 1984).

17 See, for example, Richard Sennett, *The Craftsman* (New Haven: Yale University Press, 2008), 41–45, 73–74; who suggests this underpins the modern role of the architect as generating ideas more than buildings. See also Robin Evans, *Translations from Drawing to Building and Other Essays* (Cambridge, MA: MIT Press, 1996).

18 See in particular Paola Bertucci, *Artisanal Enlightenment: Science and the Mechanical Arts in Old Regime France* (New Haven: Yale University Press, 2017).

19 Nathan Glazer, 'The Schools of the Minor Professions', *Minerva* 12:3 (1974), 346–364. His article focuses on the post-war tendency of American university programmes to incorporate professions such as teaching and social work, which were until then learned through experience and apprenticeships. Architecture is grouped with 'other' professional schools such as engineering by virtue of its reliance on technical knowledge.

20 Alva Noë, *Out of Our Heads: Why You Are Not Your Brain, and Other Lessons from the Biology of Consciousness* (New York: Farrar, Strauss and Giroux, 2009).

21 On the social dimension of tacit knowledge, see Stephen P. Turner, *The Social Theory of Practices: Tradition, Tacit Knowledge, and Presuppositions* (Chicago: University of Chicago Press, 1994); on the slippage between words, ideas and materialization, see Adrian Forty, *Words and Buildings: A Vocabulary of Modern Architecture* (London: Thames and Hudson, 2000).

22 Nathan Glazer, 'The Schools of the Minor Professions', *Minerva* 12:3 (1974), 346–364.
23 Donald A. Schön, *The Reflective Practitioner: How Professionals Think In Action* (New York: Basic Books, 1984); Donald A. Schön, *The Design Studio: An Exploration of its Traditions and Potentials* (London: RIBA Publications, 1983).
24 See, for example, Nigel Cross, 'Designerly Ways of Knowing: Design Discipline Versus Design Science', *Design Issues* 17:3 (2001), 49–55; Bryan Lawson, *How Designers Think* (London: The Architectural Press, 1980).
25 See, for example, Christopher Frayling, 'Research in Art and Design', *Royal College of Art Research Papers* 1:1 (1993), 1–5; Jeremy Till, *Architecture Depends* (Cambridge, MA: MIT Press, 2009).
26 NWO-funded startup project 'The Tacit Dimension: Architectural Knowledge and Scientific Research' (2014–2016, project no. 236-57-001).
27 ERC-funded training network 'Communities of Tacit Knowledge: Architecture and its Ways of Knowing' (2019–2023, project no. 860413).

Bibliography

Allen, Stan, *Practice: Architecture, Technique and Representation* (Amsterdam: G+B Arts International, 2000)

Bertucci, Paola, *Artisanal Enlightenment: Science and the Mechanical Arts in Old Regime France* (New Haven: Yale University Press, 2017)

Buijsman, Stefan, *AI: Alsmaar Intelligenter* (Amsterdam: De Bezige Bij, 2020)

Criado Perez, Caroline, *Invisible Women: Data Bias in a World Designed for Men* (New York: Harry N. Abrams, 2019)

Cross, Nigel, 'Designerly Ways of Knowing: Design Discipline Versus Design Science', *Design Issues* 17:3 (2001), 49–55

Evans, Robin, *Translations from Drawing to Building and Other Essays* (Cambridge, Mass: MIT Press, 1996)

Forty, Adrian, *Words and Buildings: A Vocabulary of Modern Architecture* (London: Thames and Hudson, 2000)

Frayling, Christopher, 'Research in Art and Design', *Royal College of Art Research Papers* 1:1 (1993), 1–5

Glazer, Nathan, 'The Schools of the Minor Professions', *Minerva* 12:3 (1974), 346–364.

Haraway, Donna, 'A Manifesto for Cyborgs: Science, Technology, and Socialist Feminism in the 1980s', *Socialist Review* 80 (1985), 65–107.

Haraway, Donna, 'Situated Knowledges: The Science Question in Feminism and the Privilege of Partial Perspective', *Feminist Studies* 14:3 (1988), 575–599

Hauptmann, Deborah and Warren Neidich (eds.), *Cognitive Architecture. From Biopolitics to Noopolitics. Architecture & Mind in the Age of Communication and Information* (Rotterdam: nai010publishers, 2010)

Hayles, N. Katharine, *How We Became Posthuman: Virtual Bodies in Cybernetics, Literature and Informatics* (Chicago: University of Chicago Press, 1999)

Kahneman, Daniel, Paul Slovic and Amos Tversky, *Judgment Under Uncertainty: Heuristics and Biases* (New York: Cambridge University Press, 1982)

Lawson, Bryan, *How Designers Think* (London: The Architectural Press, 1980)

Noë, Alva, *Out of Our Heads: Why You Are Not Your Brain and Other Lessons from the Biology of Consciousness* (New York: Farrar, Strauss and Giroux, 2009)

Payne, Alina A., 'Architectural History and the History of Art: A Suspended Dialogue', *Journal of the Society of Architectural Historians* 58:3 (1999), 292–299.

Polanyi, Michael, 'Tacit Knowing: Its Bearing on Some Problems of Philosophy', *Reviews of Modern Physics* 34:4 (1962), 601–616.

Polanyi, Michael, *The Tacit Dimension* (Chicago: University of Chicago Press, 1966)

Ryle, Gilbert, 'Knowing How and Knowing That: The Presidential Address', *Proceedings of the Aristotelian Society* 46:1 (1946), 1–16.

Schön, Donald A., *The Reflective Practitioner: How Professionals Think In Action* (New York: Basic Books, 1984)

Schön, Donald A., *The Design Studio: An Exploration of its Traditions and Potentials* (London: RIBA Publications, 1983)

Sennett, Richard, *The Craftsman* (New Haven: Yale University Press, 2008)

Stengers, Isabelle, 'Introductory Notes on an Ecology of Practices', *Cultural Studies Review* 11:1 (2005), 183–196

Till, Jeremy, *Architecture Depends* (Cambridge, MA: MIT Press, 2009)

Turner, Stephen P., *The Social Theory of Practices: Tradition, Tacit Knowledge, and Presuppositions* (Chicago: University of Chicago Press, 1994)

Varela, Francesco J., Evan Thompson and Eleanor Rosch, *The Embodied Mind: Cognitive Science and Human Experience.* Revised edition (Cambridge, MA: MIT Press, 2017 [orig. 1991])

Wright, Gwendolyn, 'History for Architects', in: Gwendolyn Wright and Janet Parks (eds.), *The History of History in American Schools of Architecture 1865-1975* (New York: Temple Buell and Princeton Architectural Press, 1990)

Performative Design Research: En-acting Knowledge in Teaching

Angelika Schnell

In the last few decades, the type of explorations typically identified as 'artistic research' has criticized the normativity of a 'strict logos-oriented world view',[1] which has dominated Western science since the beginning of the Enlightenment and led to 'widespread skepticism with regard to the conduciveness of corporeal experiences to theoretical thought'.[2] This method elaborates upon a notion developed in the 1960s in philosophy, sociology and scientific theory in the form of an examination of 'tacit knowing', a term coined by Michael Polanyi, which was initially deemed 'experiential knowledge'.[3] In contemporary 'embodiment' research, one proceeds from the assumption that artistic activities, with their non-linear products referring to complex interpretation and perception, can generate not only new ways of seeing but also knowledge that is consistently overlooked by research focused on *logos* and the dissecting analysis – namely primarily the sensuous-corporeal experience itself. In this sense, artistic research is not research *about* art but rather *with* art. Instead of understanding the main source of *science of art* research – the artwork itself – solely as a passive carrier of the meaning of ideas, the emphasis is placed on their physical and material reality, as well as on their interpretive and performative aspects, which also opens up new possibilities for the research of processes in architectural design that, in turn, can be directly encountered as 'active knowledge objects', both in the research and in the reception.

Design Paradigm

Of course, these sketchily outlined developments are complex and are also the subject of controversial debates. Nevertheless, it is clear that this initiates a series of consequences with regard to methodology and content that deserves closer attention. As a start, to facilitate an unbiased approach to this field and its complex relationships, in 2013, the platform History | Theory | Criticism (HTC) at the *Institut für Kunst und Architektur* (IKA) at Vienna's *Akademie der bildenden Künste* established a research project under the tutelage of Angelika Schnell, Eva Sommeregger, and Waltraud Indrist; its focus is the obvious connection between the two aforementioned developments. *Design Paradigm* examines the history of design in the twentieth and twenty-first centuries as artistic research (known in architecture as 'design-based research'); in other words, within the framework of *Design Paradigm,* the process of designing is reconstructed by means of performative formats and at the same time examined with respect to new inquiries and possibilities.[4]

The main thesis of *Design Paradigm* is that modernism in architecture has profoundly changed the practice and theory of architectural design; in light of the explosive growth of major cities at the start of the twentieth century, many architects also began to anticipatively incorporate extra-architectural forces – political, economic, social, technical, etc. – into architectural and urban design. The anticipation of change required architects to make this process itself transparent – by including the factor 'time', by including the 'new media', and by including other disciplines and techniques. In this way, architectural design became in many cases self-referential; not only were the structures and forms designed but also the processes that were to generate them.

This sort of conceptual design, in which the design itself is, as it were, designed – for it is that very part of the design that gives presence to the temporal, the scenario-like, and the changeable aspects of the design – goes beyond the Renaissance concept of the *disegno*, which assumes an ontological separation between the design concept and physical design execution, regardless of whether this refers to the design as the *a priori* or the *a posteriori* projected illustrations of a mental image of a building or an object.[5] The thesis of *Design Paradigm* is that the complex activity of designing will receive an additional inherent dimension, which, though it had always been present, now for the first time, as a conceptual dimension, becomes visible and tangible itself via the design image, time, or one or more temporal concepts.[6] To the extent that we are confronted with the design process itself – as a concept, as an outcome of structured events, as a field of possibilities, as an act – it becomes possible to recognize it and its own 'temporal form' (Ernst Cassirer) and to conduct research linked only at certain strategic points to the homogeneous and quantifiable linear time of the external world. Within its own qualitative and hermetic 'action time' (as well as its own 'action space'), the design process is not connected to the linear sequence of past, present and future.[7] Instead, it can unfold in many directions, heterogeneous and singular, which is why it is not possible to define a unified formal and/or aesthetic category of modern design as an operative model. The only similarity we can identify is the fact that an idea is no longer merely represented (shown) but performed (embodied in the here and now). In other words, the content is put into effect through the drawing itself; the distinction between conceptual idea and physical carrier of this idea is suspended. It is this observation that leads to the concept of performativity.

Performativity is a theory that appears to be well suited to deciphering the logic of the introversive 'action time' in modern architectural design. It originates in speech act theory, which was developed in the 1950s and 1960s by language philosopher John Austin.[8] The theory proceeds on the assumption that linguistic content is also linked to the physical pronunciation of that very content.

There is, of course, not one singular theory of performativity. In fact, following the linguistic theories and language-philosophy theories of John Austin and John Searle, it was above all cultural theorists and philosophers such as Judith Butler, Jacques Derrida and Sybille Krämer who grappled with performativity and, along with it, non-linguistic and consciously incorporated fictive enactments and performances. Sybille Krämer, for instance, speaks of *Blick-Akte* (literally, view-acts)[9] in which images can also be understood as performative. In the meantime, there is ample literature pointing to this construction of reality and the social character of the 'image-performance'.[10] Indeed, what stands out regarding all of the aforementioned publications is the fact that nowhere is a direct link forged between performativity and the architectural design process. Conversely, one occasionally does find a systematic correlation between architecture and performativity. What is more, the meaning of performativity is often reduced to 'staging' or 'enactment'. But theories of performativity go further; they attempt to grasp the inner logic of an act that does what it says it will, which is why we are interested in this self-referentiality that we rediscover in the modern design process.

Performative design research in teaching

This becomes particularly clear when one takes a look at the visualizations of architectural design since architectural modernism. A large number of drawings or images come into existence that appear to have a different status from the conventional design-related drawings, such as sketches or initial line drawings, and also have a different appearance. It is a matter of conceptual interpretations, which portray not so much a future condition as the process through which one arrives at that condition. Such conceptual representations are clear indications that it has become necessary to demonstrate in which manner the new architecture can master and bring about socio-political change.

To understand the inner logic of these interpretations, it is necessary to link research and teaching. At HTC, Angelika Schnell and Eva Sommeregger developed and taught three successive, theory-based design studios entitled 'Building the Design' (bachelor's, winter term 2012/2013), 'Building the Theory' (master's, summer term 2013) and 'Play Architecture' (bachelor's, winter term 2013/2014). What they had in common was the study of the architectural design process, more specifically, through its own means.

As a result, the studios were prefaced by research-based questions: How should we go about our research of the 'material epistemology' of architectural design since modernism? Which methodologies will be required? Do they exist, or must they be developed? Can artistic research, or design-based research, lead to new knowledge? The most important point of departure was the thesis holding that performative formats – critical re-enactments, animations, narratives, etc. – might be the appropriate methodologies to respond to questions related more to the process than to the results. The students in the respective studios were asked to research discrete, autonomous examples of architectural history with the same means they use in design practice, which led to such remarkable results that we decided to disseminate them. In 2016, the publication *Entwerfen Erforschen – Der "performative turn" im Architekturstudium* (literally: Researching design – the performative turn in the study of architecture) was published by Birkhäuser.[11]

'Building the Design' was the first step and, at the same time, the basis for the subsequent design studios. Conceptual images made by architects of the twentieth and twenty-first centuries were presented to the students. What the heterogeneous images have in common is that they are neither traditional design sketches nor finished drawings.

The students noticed that the visual means of the 'conceptual design images' were often borrowed from other disciplines – film and photography, theatre, dance and performance, as well as literature, comics and musical notation – in which time also plays an essential role. Le Corbusier's extensive use of new media for the design process is, for instance, renowned; the *promenade architecturale* was borne of the cinematographic notion of a body moving through space. To illustrate such movement studies, Le Corbusier employed a drawing and sketching style that brings to mind comic strips; the students Desislava Petkova and Paula

Fig. 1. Desislava Petkova and Paula Strunden reenact Le Corbusier's sketch from *La ville radieuse*. HTC-Studio 'Building the Design' (photo Angelika Schnell, Eva Sommeregger, Waltraud Indrist).

Strunden compellingly re-enacted its communicative functions in a series of frames (Fig. 1). In the process, Le Corbusier, the otherwise seemingly impenetrable art-world personage, became recognizable to the students as someone who takes parallel action: posing questions, reflecting and operative. And it became apparent that the drawing itself (a famous sketch from 'La ville radieuse') was something that had *been made*. Each detail presented itself as a precise relationship to a thought, and the comic-like sketch could be experienced in all its richness. Comparable, yet in the end quite different ventures are Alison and Peter Smithson's 'Patio & Pavilion' concept dating from 1956, reconstructed as a wild collage of past and present finds in the sense of the Smithsons' 'as-found' technique (Nadja Götze and Jasmin Schienegger, Fig. 2); Kazimir Malevich's Suprematist architectural drawings reconstructed in their two-dimensional flatness by means of three-dimensional analytical floating models (Avin Fathulla and David Rasner); and Aldo Rossi's analogous design method presented in a Rossi Theatre built by the students as an ambivalent mnemonic model (Kay Sallier and Doris Scheicher, Fig.3). The overall outcome was an exhibition of 12 different 're-enactments' that – more precisely and vividly than any conventional research – illustrate the process-based and conceptual character of design images.

The following spring semester, a small group of master's degree students reflected theoretically on the results of 'Building the Design'. Their task was not only to write an essay but also to consider how design-based research can be stored and published. One characteristic of 'performative' research is its fleetingness. It requires the presence of an audience that sees and hears the results of the design-based research during the performance because in this way, the processual aspects of the design and the sensuous thought itself become more clearly recognizable.

The students were asked to design a publication in which they could introduce their own pictorial designs in order to further develop the text contributions. The result was the book *Heterokopien*, which was later used as the layout model for the compendium *Entwerfen Erforschen*. We have selected Maximilian Müller's project about Kay Sallier and Doris Scheicher's 'Rossi-Re-enactment' to represent the students' work. Müller examines the vicinity of Roland Barthes's 'structuralist activity' to the performative method – a valuable contribution to the current research on the Design Paradigm.

Performative Design Research

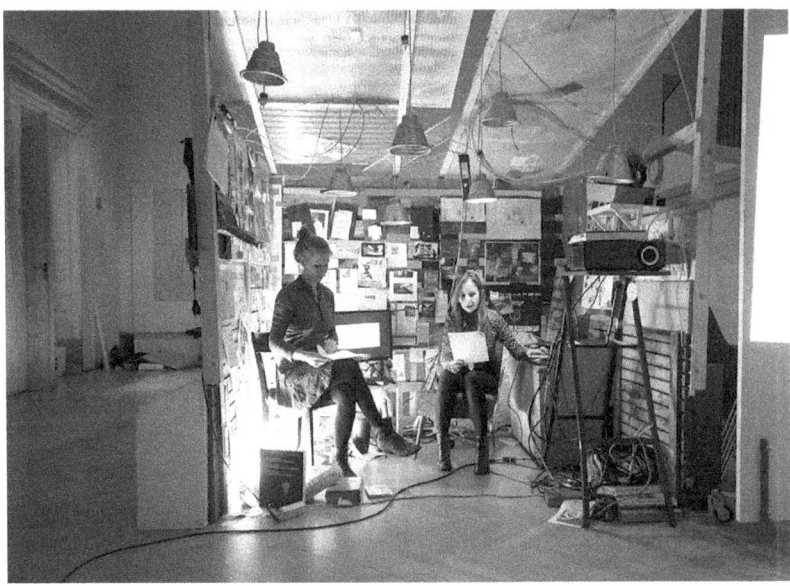

Fig. 2. Nadja Götze and Jasmin Schienegger, We Will Change, We Will Promise, surrealistic performance of the 'As Found' principle by the Smithsons. HTC-Studio 'Building the Design' (photo Angelika Schnell, Eva Sommeregger, Waltraud Indrist).

Fig. 3. *Palimpsest of Memories* is the title of Kay Sallier's and Doris Scheicher's Aldo-Rossi-theatre, here in the background as part of the final exhibition. HTC-Studio 'Building the Design' (photo Angelika Schnell).

During the autumn semester of 2013/2014, the focus was placed on the media enactment of performative design. 'Play Architecture' is based on texts that treat dwelling as a social *and* spatial phenomenon. The texts spanned from antiquity to the present day; the authors were poets, philosophers or scientists, but not architects. After selecting a book, by devising filmic designs, each student was to visualize and, at the same time, re-design the reality of the *dwelling* and *existence* described in the respective books. Some of the works provided insightful answers to the fundamental methodological question of whether a time-based design process can be more aptly expressed through moving images. Eva Herunter and Roxy Rieder's visualization of Vilém Flusser's notion of a modern world perforated by media channels employs film animation to depict something seemingly unreal, namely the constant permeation of interior and exterior, which for that very reason reveals a foundation of modern existence (Fig. 4). Fabian Puttinger, Julian Raffetseder and Jiri Tomicek rigorously translated Norbert Elias's study of court society into a modern computer game that provokes the exchangeability of spaces

Fig. 4. Vilém Flusser's writings were the blueprint for Eva Herunter's and Roxi Rieder's animation of constantly penetrated walls and windows in a Viennese Gründerzeit building block. HTC-Studio 'Play Architecture' (montage Eva Herunter, Roxi Rieder).

and costumes, and links the construction of space to the presence and actions of a proactive player. The results can indeed best be evaluated as moving images; nevertheless, in our publication, we have attempted to convey them by way of the most important sequence of images (Fig. 5).

Fig. 5. Fabian Puttinger, Julian Raffetseder and Jiri Tomicek programmed a game based on Norbert Elias' *The Court Society*. HTC-Studio 'Play Architecture' (montage Fabian Puttinger, Julian Raffetseder, Jiri Tomicek).

Two years later, another bachelor's studio looked at the performative character of teaching itself. In teaching, 'tacit knowing' has to become 'explicit knowledge'. The studio, titled 'Design the World – Keeping Up With the Bauhaus', was led by Angelika Schnell and Achim Reese.[12] It was based on the recognition that despite the huge amount of literature, the concrete teaching process of the different Bauhaus masters is hardly documented. Fragments of letters and notices of former students allowed for a (speculative) reconstruction of their education practice (Fig. 6). Based on Oskar Schlemmer's stage and theatre design (and his mechanical ballet) – bringing everyone and everything at the Bauhaus together – they sometimes literally played the Bauhaus masters' roles and by doing so, inverted the roles of teacher/jury and student, which, for instance, was performed by Svetlana Starygina, who alternately played the master Mies van der Rohe and one of his students. Another student – Lea Pflüger, performing Paul Klee – asked the audience/jury to do exercises from

Fig. 6. The audience/jury was asked to do some yoga exercises before the show started, with director Walter Gropius' (Florian Betat) complaints about the many inner and outer conflicts at the Bauhaus. HTC-Studio 'Keeping Up With the Bauhaus' (photo Angelika Schnell).

Fig. 7. One of the many enigmatic drawing exercises in Paul Klee's *Pädagogisches Skizzenbuch*, performed by Lea Pflüger (left). Svetlana Starygina explains the authoritarian didactics of Ludwig Mies van der Rohe (right). HTC-Studio 'Keeping Up With the Bauhaus' (photos Angelika Schnell).

Fig. 8. Duha Samir (together with her partner Maximilian Klammer) dances the colour circle of Gertrud Grunow, a lesser-known teacher at the Bauhaus. HTC-Studio 'Keeping Up With the Bauhaus' (photo Angelika Schnell).

his famous *Pedagogical Sketchbook*, which convincingly demonstrated the difficulties of understanding and even executing the partly confusing writing by Klee (Fig. 7). In the meantime, students Nadja Krause and Lisa Ungerhofer, both disguised as 'mechanical figures', guided the audience to a place where they should do a short yoga course. Physical exercises and the embodiment of artistic processes were an essential part of Johannes Itten's teaching programme. Hence, his famous 'Vorkurs' might be seen as an immediate introduction to 'tacit knowing'. The students Maximilian Klammer and Duha Samir even visited the last surviving students of the Bauhaus pedagogy in Geneva, with its sometimes quite esoteric teaching programmes (Fig. 8). Additionally, the audience listened to a reading by Ludwig Hilberseimer (Ella Felber), saw an electronic light show inspired by László Moholy-Nagy (Lukas Strigl) and followed a press conference of a (fictive) detective performed by Jakob Grabher, who desperately wanted to investigate the disappearance of Theo van Doesburg, who secretly established a counter-Bauhaus in Weimar.

The jury tried – unsuccessfully – to understand and master the confusing colour and form theories of Kandinsky, which opens up the question: What are our own limitations as professionals? How often do we cheat ourselves or others when we are referring to those masters, without ever looking so precisely at the material? Equally important was the fact that the students dared to face authority: the monument of famous names. They learned to criticize them in a way that, at the same time, maintained both a certain respect and a sense of curiosity.

Conclusion

The student work constitutes an important contribution to the design-based and 'performative' research of modern architectural design and design processes, by making the material directly accessible in the form of events perceptible to the senses. This method has mimetic content but does not involve mere copies; it is not so much a matter of analysing the given material – instead, it is about adding a new level of meaning to it. That also has to do with a particularity of this research: the fleetingness of performance. It requires the presence and interaction of an audience that sees and hears the results of the design-based research during the performance because in this way, processual aspects of the design and the sensuous thought itself become more clearly recognizable. As a 'practical aesthetic', it transcends the conventional boundaries between science and art and thereby referring back to the dual nature of the artistic work itself. But ultimately, through this research, the historiography of architecture will no longer be only the history of buildings but also of diverse and complex design processes. Through design-based research and, in particular, through performative methods, former passive sources become active objects of knowing.

Notes

1. Gesa Ziemer, *Verletzbare Orte. Entwurf einer praktischen Ästhetik* (Zürich/Berlin: Diaphanes, 2008), 12.
2. Undine Eberlein, 'Introduction' in: Undine Eberlein (ed.), *Zwischenleiblichkeit und bewegtes Verstehen. Incorporeity, Movement and Tacit Knowledge* (Bielefeld: transcript, 2016), 10.
3. Michael Polanyi, *The Tacit Dimension* (Chicago/London: The University of Chicago Press, 2009 [orig. 1966]). Different authors give a summary – from a sociological standpoint – of how tacit knowledge pertains to science and technology in 'Epistemologie der Ungewißheit', in: Ulrich Beck and Wolfgang Bonß (eds.), *Die Modernisierung der Moderne* (Frankfurt am Main: Suhrkamp, 2001), Chapter 2.
4. www.designparadigm.net/portfolio/building-the-design/ (last accessed 18 December, 2020).
5. See especially Erwin Panofsky, *Idea. Ein Beitrag zur Begriffsgeschichte der* älteren *Kunsttheorie* (Berlin: Verlag Volker Spiess, 1993), 23–38.
6. Karin Gloy, *Zeit. Eine Morphologie* (Freiburg/Munich: Verlag Karl Alber, 2006); Johannes Myssok and Ludger Schwarte (eds.), *Zeitstrukturen. Techniken der Vergegenwärtigung in Wissenschaft und Kunst*, (Berlin: Reimer Verlag, 2013).
7. Gloy, *Zeit*, 73–87.
8. John Austin, *How to Do Things With Words*, The William James lectures delivered at Harvard University in 1955 (Oxford: Oxford University Press, 1975 [orig. 1962]).
9. Sybille Krämer, 'Gibt es eine Performanz des Bildlichen? Reflexionen über Blickakte', in: Ludger Schwarte (ed.), *Bild-Performanz* (Munich: Wilhelm Fink Verlag, 2011), 63–90.
10. Schwarte (ed.), *Bild-Performanz*; Erika Fischer-Lichte, *Performativität* (Bielefeld: transcript, 2012); Doris Bachmann-Medick, *Cultural Turns. Neuorientierungen in den Kulturwissenschaften* (Reinbek bei Hamburg: Rowohlt, 2006); Uwe Wirth (ed.), *Performanz. Zwischen Sprachphilosophie und Kulturwissenschaften* (Frankfurt am Main: Suhrkamp, 2002).
11. Angelika Schnell, Eva Sommeregger and Waltraud Indrist (eds.), *Entwerfen Erforschen. Der 'performative turn' im Architekturstudium* (Basel/Berlin: Birkhäuser Verlag, 2016).
12. www.designparadigm.net/portfolio/design-the-world-keeping-up-with-the-bauhaus/ (last accessed 18 December, 2020).

Bibliography

Austin, John, *How to Do Things With Words*, The William James Lectures delivered at Harvard University in 1955 (Oxford: Oxford University Press, 1975 [orig. 1962])

Bachmann-Medick, Doris, *Cultural Turns. Neuorientierungen in den Kulturwissenschaften* (Reinbek bei Hamburg: Rowohlt, 2006)

Beck, Ulrich and Wolfgang Bonß (eds.), *Die Modernisierung der Moderne* (Frankfurt am Main: Suhrkamp, 2001)

Eberlein, Undine, 'Introduction', in: Undine Eberlein (ed.), *Zwischenleiblichkeit und bewegtes Verstehen. Incorporeity, Movement and Tacit Knowledge* (Bielefeld: transcript, 2016)

Fischer-Lichte, Erika, *Performativität* (Bielefeld: transcript, 2012)

Gloy, Karin, *Zeit. Eine Morphologie* (Freiburg/Munich: Verlag Karl Alber, 2006)

Krämer, Sybille, 'Gibt es eine Performanz des Bildlichen? Reflexionen über Blickakte', in: Ludger Schwarte (ed.), *Bild-Performanz* (Munich: Wilhelm Fink Verlag, 2011), 63–90

Myssok, Johannes and Ludger Schwarte (eds.), *Zeitstrukturen. Techniken der Vergegenwärtigung in Wissenschaft und Kunst*, (Berlin: Reimer Verlag, 2013)

Panofsky, Erwin, *Idea. Ein Beitrag zur Begriffsgeschichte der älteren Kunsttheorie* (Berlin: Verlag Volker Spiess, 1993)

Polanyi, Michael, *The Tacit Dimension* (Chicago/London: The University of Chicago Press, 2009 [orig. 1966]).

Schnell, Angelika, Eva Sommeregger and Waltraud Indrist (eds.), *Entwerfen Erforschen. Der 'performative turn' im Architekturstudium* (Basel/Berlin: Birkhäuser Verlag, 2016)

Schnell et al., Project 'Design Paradigm', www.designparadigm.net/

Schwarte, Ludger (ed.), *Bild-Performanz* (Munich: Wilhelm Fink Verlag, 2011)

Wirth, Uwe (ed.), *Performanz. Zwischen Sprachphilosophie und Kulturwissenschaften* (Frankfurt m Main: Suhrkamp, 2002)

Ziemer, Gesa, *Verletzbare Orte. Entwurf einer praktischen Ästhetik* (Zürich/Berlin: Diaphanes, 2008)

Teaching Architecture Full Scale

Mari Lending

For centuries, plaster casts have been crucial to the training of architects. Their role in education becomes particularly vivid when examined through the lens of the transition from one paradigmatic pedagogical system to another. When versions of Bauhaus pedagogy began to displace Beaux-Arts teaching, plaster casts were banished. Yet their subsequent recuperation also complicates overly simplistic renderings of these transitions (Fig.1).

An ample architecture collection was required for the founding of the first American school of architecture at the Massachusetts Institute of Technology. Thousands of objects and 400 plaster casts, mostly smaller building fragments used for teaching in ornament, were part of the multimedia Museum of Architectural Appliances that its first professor of architecture, William Ware had purchased in Europe.[1] At Harvard University, bigger casts more vividly displayed spatial and architectural qualities. The Harvard collection serves as a good example for complicating simplistic explanations of the transition to a new pedagogical regime. Beaux-Arts-trained Joseph Hudnut was 'the first to attack the French system in a decisive way' when appointed dean at the architecture school at Harvard in 1936. As Dean of the School of Architecture at Columbia University, Hudnut had already done away with the cast collection in New York. At Harvard, he reorganized the Faculty of Architecture into the Graduate School of Design (GSD), sweeping away the Beaux-Arts teaching methods and implementing new programmes corresponding to the needs of modern life.[2]

Fig. 1. Egyptian reliefs, stairwell. Courtesy of Yale School of Architecture, 2017.

At Yale, one particular Bauhaus protagonist had hands-on involvement in the discarding of the biggest and finest cast collection in an American university. When appointed the first chair of the new Department of Design in 1950 – at what, in 1864, had been established as the Yale School of Fine Arts – Josef Albers made it clear 'that the French Beaux-Arts casts had no place in the methods of the German Bauhaus'.³ It was, though, a much-welcomed iconoclasm that took place in New Haven. The Dean of the school, who had tempted Albers to leave Black Mountain College for Yale, described his arrival as a revolution: 'the art school at Yale needed a little shaking up, a little different perspective', he said, stressing that 'one has to know design, not only copy models and plaster casts'.⁴

When Albers arrived in New Haven, Street Hall, the school's first premises, was drowning in one of its main pedagogical tools. The matter had already been addressed in the 1890s: 'On their arrival from abroad they were placed throughout the building wherever there was available space', the dean then reported, addressing the want of space for the rapidly expanding collection of plaster casts.⁵ One can only imagine how sordid this historicist monument to Beaux-Arts training must have appeared to a Bauhaus teacher and easily understand his compulsion to get rid of the casts, which signified exercises in historical emulation and appropriation of tradition by repetition and imitation. 'Too much history leaves little room for work', Albers claimed in an essay published while he was still teaching in Weimar. 'Historisch oder Jetzig?' – 'Historical or Contemporary' – launched a number of issues that Albers would rehearse and refine in countless articles and lectures for half a century. Traditional art education was 'at least three hundred years behind the times' and all about 'note-taking and copying', while the Bauhaus aimed at reintegrating art education and practical action 'into harmony with the actual demands of contemporary life'.⁶ In 1950, the Beaux-Arts cobwebs were dusted off when both 'fine' and 'art' disappeared from the school's name, and the School of Architecture and Design was divided into three departments: Architecture, Design and Drama. 'Albers came and shook it up. Blood was spilt and feathers flew', as an eyewitness, a professor in art history later recalled: Albers 'literally threw the casts out on High Street. They were very old. Probably 100 years old. It just happened overnight'.⁷

Yet in this case, it is less the destruction than the salvaging of some of the casts that comes as a surprise, namely Paul Rudolph's recovery of the remnants that he 're-excavated from the bowels of Yale', as he put it, and the way he mounted the casts across the nine floors and 37 levels of his Art and Architecture building, inaugurated in 1963 – as an unforeseen constellation of cast concrete and plaster casts.[8] Rudolph's repurposing of an old Beaux-Arts collection into a brutalist structure again complicates simplistic dichotomies of historicism versus modernism.

While designing the new school, Rudolph was highly preoccupied with the unfulfilled potential of the Beaux-Arts and the *cul-de-sac* of modern architecture, 'limited now to goldfish bowls, buildings on stilts, and the efforts of structural exhibitionists', as he polemicized when assuming the chairmanship of the Department of Architecture at Yale in February 1958.[9] Commissioned to design a new building for the school, Rudolph found himself in the same position as Schinkel in Berlin, Gropius in Dessau and Mies in Chicago, namely to design a school he himself was to direct, with the prospect of presenting a pedagogic vision in built form. The casts played a critical role in this vision, as a possibility for teaching architecture at full scale and presenting a built history lesson with several unexpected twists.

Public instruction

In the nineteenth century, architectural casts meandered out of schools and into the public sphere. Displaying architecture from across time and place, these plaster monuments were used to teach architecture history at full scale and in three dimensions to new museum audiences on both sides of the Atlantic. The distinction between school collections and public displays is, however, not easily drawn. Schools could be quite public places, and some architecture schools became important suppliers of casts for museums. Common to the different curatorial and didactic arrangements in museums was the ambition to present architecture as a profoundly historical phenomenon, relative to time and place. In different constellations, full-scale monuments were organized as history lessons in nineteenth-century obsessions such as style, comparison, nation, evolution and, not least, *chronology*.

At the relocated Crystal Palace at Sydenham, the 10 architecture courts opened in 1854 made the first and most ambitious attempt to display architecture as an evolutionary, progressive history. The courts spanned from Assyria and Egypt to the Renaissance and allowed the audience to promenade through time and place, experiencing a spatial history of monuments. The South Kensington Museum was instrumental in igniting the international production and exchange of architectural casts from the 1860s onwards. The architecture courts were tailored to house awe-inspiring monuments and aimed at presenting an emerging global history of architecture that could be experienced spatially, synoptically and simultaneously. In Paris, the *Musée de Sculpture Comparée* opened for the public in 1882. Often discussed as a national endeavour, the scope was, however, more ambitious in its audacious temporal transplantation of Winckelmann's theory of the development of Greek art to French soil. By translating the fundamentals of classical art into a national trajectory in the curation of French monuments across time, it implied a veritable relativization of the classical absolute.

Many cast museums bordered between schools and museums, aiming at training students on the one hand and the public on the other. The Architectural Museum in London, established in 1851, was always discussed as a teaching tool. Among its founders were a number of central players in British architectural culture, including John Ruskin, Charles Cockerell, Owen Jones and George Godwin, editor of *The Builder*. The purpose of this collection of thousands of small architectural fragments was to give students of architecture and 'art-workmen an opportunity of studying reproductions of works, the originals of which neither their time nor means would allow them to visit'.[10] In fact, these nineteenth-century cast collections were often discussed as a surrogate for the grand tour and as a democratization of this aristocratic, educational institution. This was even the case for a collection that sprung directly from elitist grand tour culture, namely Sir John Soane's home museum in London, which served as a teaching collection for Professor Soane's students at the Royal Academy in the first decades of the century. Soane brought his students to his home every week to study monuments in depth and, as Soane put it in 1812, the casts gave students without 'means of visiting Greece and Italy some better ideas of ancient Works than would be conveyed thro: the medium of drawings or prints'.[11] Another inverted Grand Tour took place in Paris, where in the 1870s, architect Felix Duban covered the courtyard of the École des Beaux-Arts with a glass ceiling to house full-scale editions of the north-west corner of the Parthenon and two of the three columns of the ruined colonnade of the Temple of Castor and Pollux at the Roman Forum, flooded in natural light. Duban stressed the importance of the students, in their everyday teaching environment, experiencing the two most canonical specimens of the Doric and Corinthian orders in their *'dimensions réelles'*.[12]

A shared sentiment of these architecture collections was that the study of full-scale reproduction in galleries provided a better understanding than architecture does in situ. This emphasis on the importance of students experiencing architecture in its real dimensions became the ideal for the full-scale plaster monuments in museums in Europe and the USA. Yet while the École des Beaux-Arts used the casts to teach the timeless beauty and universal value of the great monuments of antiquity, timeliness – architecture's dependence on time and place – became the paradigm for most museums' striving to display perfect plaster chronologies and teach history full scale.

Learning in mysterious ways

Paul Rudolph was himself Beaux-Arts trained at the Alabama Polytechnic Institute, before studying with Gropius at the GSD. Looking back, in the early 1950s, he pondered: 'in 1941 there was a sense of urgency at Harvard. Most had lost faith in the Beaux Arts system, but what was to fill the vacuum?'[13] Throughout the 1950s, musings on the unfulfilled potentials of the Beaux-Arts that had been lost with modernism were ubiquitous in his writings.

Upon his arrival in New Haven in 1958, Rudolph published an article in the Yale journal *Perspecta* that anticipated the ethos of the Art and Architecture Building:

> We need desperately to relearn that art of disposing our buildings to create different kinds of space: the quiet, enclosed, isolated, shaded space: the hustling, bustling space, pungent with vitality; the paved, dignified, vast, sumptuous, even awe-inspiring space; the mysterious space; the transition space which defines, separates, and yet juxtaposes spaces of contrasting character. We need sequences of space which

arouse one's curiosity, give a sense of anticipation, which beckon and impel us to rush forward to find that releasing space which dominates, which acts as a climax and magnet, and gives direction.[14]

It reads as a manifesto, and hardly anything written on the Art and Architecture Building (or A&A Building) sums up its spatial qualities more precisely than these lines. With an ensemble of recovered Assyrian, Egyptian, Greek and medieval works, Rudolph indeed turned the new school's narrow, enclosed, anti-monumental stairwell into a transitional space that is awe-inspiring, mysterious and anticipation-inciting, letting the casts provide focal points while making the mundane function of vertical circulation a sensual experience. Rudolph's unexpected and incredibly untimely introduction of the casts allowed these qualities to become manifest as experienced space.

Somehow, Yale was the perfect place for Rudolph's rethinking of the overlooked potentials of Beaux-Art pedagogies. From its establishment in the 1860s, the Yale School of Fine Arts offered a rigorous Beaux-Arts education with a curriculum fashioned after the École des Beaux-Arts in Paris. The students sketched from casts every morning for two years, and until the 1940s, the American Prix de Rome was dubbed Prix de Yale in common parlance. For the inauguration of Street Hall in 1869, a number of exquisite casts were in place, most of which had been ordered from Paris. From the very beginning, this collection was founded on an explicitly historicist outlook, intended to document the great periods. New works were constantly incorporated from a number of sources, made from moulds struck from the originals in Athens, the Uffizi, the Vatican, the Louvre, the British Museum and so forth. They were thus considered authentic, authorized works. The collection was constantly updated in parallel with archaeological excavation.

The Art and Architecture Building is monumental and itself a monument to materiality. The building's characteristic corrugated concrete surfaces were the result of a labour-intensive endeavour. Aggregate was poured into vertically ribbed moulds, and after 24 hours, the striated concrete was meticulously hand-hammered, resulting in particular optical, haptic and tactile effects. Inside and outside, the surface texture, the continuously ridged surface of coarse concrete, allows for a dramatic play of light and shadow through the day. Rudolph's interest in light and shadow, in weathering and optical delight, was highlighted in the layering of casts on the cast concrete walls. The weatherability of both concrete and plaster, and the material historicity of the casts – themselves manifesting a range of techniques of patination – added texture, nuance, colour and atmosphere to the building. Across the floating spaces, the casts distinctively punctuated vastness with intimacy. The works, Rudolph explained, were used 'to reduce the scale of the interiors, which is, I believe, the basic relationship between all ornament and architectural space'.[15]

Rudolph came across the casts that Albers did not get to destroy accidentally while designing the A&A Building. In the basement of Street Hall, he even retrieved casts that were still in their crates and, thus, brand-new, unseen novelties, appearing as time capsules when premiered in 1963. Among these uncrated casts was an incredibly rare piece produced on site at the female pharaoh Hatshepsut's funerary temple in the Theban necropolis in 1907, commissioned by the Metropolitan Museum of Art and made in three editions. Across the concrete structure, the casts twisted and enhanced perceptions of horizontality and verticality, nowhere more strikingly than in the audacious mounting of the brand-new Egyptian bas-reliefs. Both in its ancient, original version and as a cast, the narrative was played out in the horizontal, documenting in amazing detail an expedition to Punt in East Africa during the Eighteenth Dynasty, that is, in the fifteenth century BCE.

The polychrome relief came in 200 pieces to be laboriously joined together. Rudolph, however, installed the work at five different locations, to very different effects. 'They were used at the stairway', he said, taking advantage of the vertical possibilities proposed by the many pieces, 'because they were quite vertical, they start at the stairs and come up into the more brilliantly lit space so it goes from dark to light'.[16] Here, the architect refers to the monumental, vertical hanging of 72 pieces on the double-height wall on the fifth and sixth floors. On the fourth floor, he hung 12 pieces depicting trees in a completely abstracted way that allows for a close look at the ancient Egyptian vegetation. Five pieces depicting an Egyptian vessel in detail were hung as an individual artwork over a sofa in a little lounge one passes when heading toward the roof terrace. Over the years, many of the panels were lost or wrecked, due to vandalism and neglect.

In the early 1960s, Rudolph inventively used the remaining fragments to accentuate the transition from a darker to a lighter plateau in the glamorous penthouse overlooking the Yale campus, where the deep orange carpet used all over the building makes the Egyptian wall glow. Today, 148 out of 200 fragments of this rare piece – what had survived the course of time before the restoration of both the building and the casts in 2008 – appear as a ruin of a ruin, extensively perforated and thus revealing the concrete relief background, having attained an eerily contemporary feel. Rudolph used the Beaux-Arts objects in a strikingly architectural way. They helped modulate space and define scale, while their materiality and

Fig. 2. Library reading room with panels from Luca della Robbia's Cantoria. Courtesy of Yale School of Architecture, 2017.

colour in juxtaposition to the play of light and shadow on the concrete walls, heightened the material perception of the spaces. Together they aimed at bringing out what Rudolph described as the 'unique forms inherent in every material'.[17]

On the school's 25th anniversary, Rudolph reiterated how he sought to build his pedagogical ideals into the structure: 'I believe that you learn about things in mysterious ways, and that the chance encounter can be as important as the formal lecture', he declared.

The mounting of the casts throughout the building was meant to foster surprises and unexpected exposés. These chance encounters happened in many ways. Still, today, those who spend time in the building will experience how the recurrent discovery of the fragments come as a surprise. Most surprising of all is their unceremonious presence – they are simply there. For instance, three panels from Pausanias's high relief frieze of the temple of Apollo at Bassae, cast from the originals in the British Museum, are mounted in the rear gallery in Hastings Hall, easily overlooked. Nine of the 10 panels from Luca della Robbia's Cantoria from the cathedral in Florence float high above the floor in the library (Fig. 2). Deprived of the balcony that serves as their architectural frame, they are mounted in their original order, with the two side panels flanking the two series and an empty space left for one lost piece. Above the table in the seminar room, Greeks and Amazons are fighting on the Amazonomachy frieze from the Mausoleum of Halicarnassus.

History lessons

Strikingly, Rudolph's school was interpreted as a personal effort, even as a self-portrait, and its immediate reception reads as something of a Freudian, exceedingly gendered, (homo)sexual psychodrama in which haptic, tactile and optic effects, as well as sensual, physical and perceptual qualities, were persistently conflated with the architect's persona and personality.[18] Characterized as 'iconoclastic' and 'individualistic', the building was seen as the culmination of Rudolph's architectural philosophy to date: 'an architecture in which the personality of the designer decidedly asserts itself'.[19] As interesting as this conflation of an architect and his architecture is, the question remains what kind of history lesson and architectural philosophy might be lingering in the pairing of cast concrete and plaster casts. Vincent Scully once described Rudolph as a 'physical historian' who dealt with historical problems, with 'the past and, a function of the past, with the future'.[20] When looking at the A&A Building through the lens of the casts, a radical physical history emerges.

Rudolph's mounting of the casts was not intended to display historical narratives. His installation of historical artefacts was completely detached from the original collection's idiom of forming a canon of masterpieces and the will to demonstrate historical systems by style, nation, evolution and comparison. Reintroducing these obsolete pedagogical tools in a school building was not intended to provide a lesson in nineteenth-century conceptions of history. Rudolph treated these *objets trouvés* as precious originals, as rare artefacts from an abandoned paradigm, and installed them so that each piece might produce its full effect upon the spectator.

In fact, they belong to a wider consideration of history and temporalities, played out in different objects with times of their own. A few contemporary artworks were commissioned for the new school, among them a steel sculpture by Josef Albers installed above the entrance. Contemporary with the artworks of the 1960s were the Sullivan casts which blended seamlessly with the old casts. As the A&A Building was under construction, the demolition of Penn Station in New York City was underway, while Louis Sullivan's 1892 Garrick Theatre in Chicago was also demolished: two seminal events in modern American preservation (Fig. 3). Before the Sullivan building was torn down, its most ornamental parts were cast, for documentation. As such, the Sullivan pieces were novelties in 1963. Rudolph mounted 30 panels, painted white, in two sections. Juxtaposing the Sullivan frieze with metopes from the south wall of the Parthenon showing Greeks are battling Centaurs, he expanded the canon in its cast trajectory, including the recent past by invoking contemporary debates and failures in the field of preservation.

The shimmering of the concrete walls comes from corals that were blended into the aggregate. Together with the scallop shell inserted in the concrete wall next to a little Gothic saint in the narrow stairway on the first floor, as well as another shell hidden in the sub-basement, the sediments and fossils open an immense time span in the brutalist structure, which might evoke the *longue durée* that Fernand Braudel termed geographical, geological and even oceanic time (Fig. 4). Delays, as in the

Fig. 3. Sullivan frieze and Parthenon metopes along concrete beams. Courtesy of Yale School of Architecture, 2017.

Fig. 4. Scallop shell and Gothic saint, 2016 (photo Mari Lending).

resurfacing of the fresh Egyptian bas-relief, and obsolescence empowered the resurrected collection.

In New Haven, the mounting of frescos, friezes, metopes, capitals and other architectural elements took on the form of a Bakhtinian chronotope. Fused into a carefully thought-out concrete whole, 'time, as it were, thickens, takes on flesh, becomes artistically visible; likewise, space becomes charged and responsive to the movements of time, plot and history', to anachronistically let Bakhtin's chronotopicity frame the effect of how these fractured temporalities articulated spaces of a weird contemporaneity.[21]

Because 'each piece was roughly the same size it made a kind of checkerboard pattern and became all of a sudden familiar and very modern', said the architect about the placing of casts in the stairwell, such as the vertical stacking of the Parthenon frieze – famous for its proto-cinematic horizontality – on the wall of a narrow, double-height stairway (Fig. 5).

Fig 5. Vertically stacked Parthenon frieze in stairwell, 2006, before 2008 replacement. Courtesy of Yale School of Architecture.

Two rare Assyrian casts (made before the British Museum banned more reproductions of their Assyrian collection in the 1880s, and once much demanded works) and the Egyptian, Greek and Medieval works in this enclosure together form a condensed, yet splintered, historical spectacle. Rudolph's mounting was polychronic, not chronological. Dehistoricized as the casts were, their historicity became legible. This built pedagogy forms a history lesson on a derelict pedagogical regime, letting devaluated relics emerge as contemporary within their new architectural framework.

Albers removed the casts for pedagogical reasons. Rudolph incorporated them into the building as part of his programme for the training of architecture students. While from a Bauhaus perspective, the casts could only connote backwardness, in Rudolph's built vision, they pointed to history in the service of the present and the future. 'Josef didn't like the history of this or that', according to Vincent Scully; both 'his strength and his limitation was his Bauhaus approach to things'.[22] 'I believe that the rather purist arguments against using the casts are outweighed by the effect of their 'presence' in a building devoted to learning', said Rudolph.[23] He was clearly not aiming at re-establishing a timeless, classicist aesthetic or displaying the casts as a matter of style, comparison or chronology. That would have been both anachronistic and meaningless.

In Rudolph's scheme, Albers' persistent dichotomy of 'Historical or Contemporary' was resolved – when the fragile objects were relaunched as both historical and contemporary.

Notes

1. Mark Wigley, 'Prosthetic Theory: The Disciplining of Architecture', *Assemblage* 15 (August 1991), 6–29.
2. Jill Pearlman, *Inventing American Modernism: Joseph Hudnut, Walter Gropius, and the Bauhaus Legacy at Harvard* (Charlottesville: University of Virginia Press, 2007), 1.
3. Betsy Fahlman, 'A Plaster of Paris Antiquity: Nineteenth Century Cast Collections', *Southeastern College Art Conference Review* 12:1 (1991), 9.
4. Frederick A. Horowitz, 'Charles H. Sawyer Discusses Josef Albers. A Conversation with Fred Horowitz February 12, 2000', 1. Box 1, 3. Archives of the Josef and Anni Albers Foundation, Bethany, Connecticut. Hereafter, Fred Horowitz papers.
5. John Ferguson Weir, 'The Yale Collection of Casts', 1. Undated lecture manuscript, probably turn of the century. John Ferguson Weir Papers (MS 550), Manuscripts and Archives, Yale University Library.

6   Josef Albers, 'Historical or Contemporary' (1924), Russel Stockman (transl.), in: Nicholas Fox Weber and Jeannette Redensek (eds.), *Josef Albers: Minimal Means, Maximum Effect* (Madrid: Fundación Juan March, 2014), 207–8. See also Brenda Danilowitz, 'Teaching Design: A Short History of Joseph Albers', in: Frederick A. Horowitz and Brenda Danilowitz, *Josef Albers: To Open Eyes. The Bauhaus, Black Mountain College, and Yale* (London: Phaidon, 2006).
7   Frederick A. Horowitz, 'Notes on a Conversation with George Heard Hamilton and Polly Hamilton at Williamstown June 3, 1992', 2. Box 1. Fred Horowitz papers.
8   Paul Rudolph quoted in 'A & A: Yale School of Art and Architecture; Paul Rudolph, Architect', *Progressive Architecture* 45 (February 1964), 115.
9   Rudolph's inaugural speech appeared as 'Architecture: The Unending Search', *Yale Alumni Magazine* 21:8 (May 1958). Reprinted as 'Alumni Day Speech: Yale School of Architecture, February 1958', *Oppositions* 4 (1974), 142–143.
10 'Fine Arts', *Illustrated London News* (24 July 1867), 90.
11 John Soane, 'Crude Hints towards a History of My House in L[incoln's] I[nn] Fields', in: Helen Dorey (ed.), *Visions of Ruin: Architectural Fantasies and Designs for Garden Follies* (London: Sir John Soane's Museum, 1999), 69.
12 Christiane Pinatel, 'La "Restauration" en plâtre de deux colonnes du temple de Castor et Pollux dans la Petit écurie Royale de Versailles: Histoire et archéologie', *Revue Archéologique* 1:35 (January 2003), 74.
13 Paul Rudolph, 'Paul Rudolph', *Perspecta* 1 (Summer 1952), 19.
14 Rudolph, 'Alumni Day Speech', 142. This passage appeared almost verbatim in 'The Six Determinants of Architectural Form', *Architectural Record* 120 (October 1956), 183–190; and in 'To Enrich Our Architecture', *Journal of Architectural Education* 13:1 (Spring 1958), 9–12.
15 Rudolph quoted in 'A & A: Yale School of Art and Architecture', 115.
16 C. Ray Smith, 'Interview no. 7 with Paul Rudolph, 1977', 5–6. C. Ray Smith Files on the Yale Art and Architecture Building by Paul Rudolph. Box 1. Manuscripts and Archives, Yale University Library.
17 Ibid., 5–6.
18 Timothy M. Rohan, 'Rendering the Surface: Paul Rudolph's Art and Architecture Building at Yale', *Grey Room* 1 (Autumn 2000), 84–107.
19 Ilse M. Reese and James T. Burns Jr., 'The Opposites: Expressionism and Formalism at Yale', *Progressive Architecture* 45 (February 1964), 128.
20 Vincent Scully, *American Architecture and Urbanism* (London: Thames and Hudson, 1969), 257.
21 Mikhail Bakhtin, 'Forms of Time and of the Chronotope in the Novel: Notes towards a Historical Poetics' (1937–38), in: Carol Emerson and Michael Holquist (transl.), *The Dialogic Imagination* (Austin: University of Texas Press, 1982), 84.
22 Frederick A. Horowitz, 'Vincent Scully Discusses Josef Albers. A Conversation with Fred Horowitz, December 9, 1995', 10. Fred Horowitz papers.
23 Rudolph quoted in 'A & A: Yale School of Art and Architecture', 115.

Bibliography

'A & A: Yale School of Art and Architecture; Paul Rudolph, Architect', *Progressive Architecture* 45 (February 1964), 109–127

Albers, Josef, 'Historical or Contemporary' (1924), transl. Russel Stockman, in: Nicholas Fox Weber and Jeannette Redensek (eds.), *Josef Albers: Minimal Means, Maximum Effect* (Madrid: Fundación Juan March, 2014), 207–8.

Bakhtin, Mikhail, 'Forms of Time and of the Chronotope in the Novel: Notes Towards a Historical Poetics' (1937–38), in: Carol Emerson and Michael Holquist (transl.), *The Dialogic Imagination* (Austin: University of Texas Press, 1982), 84–258.

Danilowitz, Brenda, 'Teaching Design: A Short History of Josef Albers', in: Frederick A. Horowitz and Brenda Danilowitz, *Josef Albers: To Open Eyes. The Bauhaus, Black Mountain College, and Yale* (London: Phaidon, 2006)

Fahlman, Betsy, 'A Plaster of Paris Antiquity: Nineteenth Century Cast Collections', *Southeastern College Art Conference Review* 12:1 (1991), 1–9.

'Fine Arts', *Illustrated London News* (24 July 1867)

Horowitz, Frederick A., Fred Horowitz papers, Archives of the Josef and Anni Albers Foundation, Bethany, Connecticut

Horowitz, Frederick A. and Brenda Danilowitz, *Josef Albers: To Open Eyes. The Bauhaus, Black Mountain College, and Yale* (London: Phaidon, 2006)

Pearlman, Jill, *Inventing American Modernism: Joseph Hudnut, Walter Gropius, and the Bauhaus Legacy at Harvard* (Charlottesville: University of Virginia Press, 2007)

Pinatel, Christiane, 'La "Restauration" en plâtre de deux colonnes du temple de Castor et Pollux dans la Petit écurie Royale de Versailles: Histoire et Archéologie', *Revue Archéologique* 1:35 (January 2003), 67–114

Reese, Ilse M. and James T. Burns Jr., 'The Opposites: Expressionism and Formalism at Yale', *Progressive Architecture* 45 (February 1964), 128–129

Rohan, Timothy M., 'Rendering the Surface: Paul Rudolph's Art and Architecture Building at Yale', *Grey Room* 1 (Autumn 2000), 84–107

Rudolph, Paul, 'Paul Rudolph', *Perspecta* 1 (Summer 1952), 18–25

Rudolph, Paul, 'The Six Determinants of Architectural Form', *Architectural Record* 120 (October 1956), 183–190

Rudolph, Paul, 'Architecture: The Unending Search', *Yale Alumni Magazine* 21:8 (May 1958)

Rudolph, Paul, 'To Enrich Our Architecture', *Journal of Architectural Education* 13:1 (Spring 1958), 9–12

Rudolph, Paul, 'Alumni Day Speech: Yale School of Architecture, February 1958', *Oppositions* 4 (1974), 142

Scully, Vincent, *American Architecture and Urbanism* (London: Thames and Hudson, 1969)

Smith, C. Ray, 'Interview No. 7 with Paul Rudolph, 1977', C. Ray Smith Files on the Yale Art and Architecture Building by Paul Rudolph. Box 1. Manuscripts and Archives, Yale University Library

Soane, John, 'Crude Hints towards a History of My House in L[incoln's] I[nn] Fields', in: Helen Dorey (ed.), *Visions of Ruin: Architectural Fantasies and Designs for Garden Follies* (London: Sir John Soane's Museum, 1999), 53–59

Weir, John Ferguson 'The Yale Collection of Casts', undated lecture manuscript. John Ferguson Weir Papers (MS 550), Manuscripts and Archives, Yale University Library.

Weber, Nicholas Fox and Jeannette Redensek (eds.), *Josef Albers: Minimal Means, Maximum Effect* (Madrid: Fundación Juan March, 2014)

Wigley, Mark, 'Prosthetic Theory: The Disciplining of Architecture', *Assemblage* 15 (August 1991), 6–29

Transformative Dialogues: On Material Knowing in Architecture

Eireen Schreurs

> Labrouste was the first who understood the advantages of the use of iron, not as a framework, hidden in old forms, but as a new means of construction that could be frankly revealed in a new form.[1]
> M. Rapine, architect, 1910

In 1857, the architect Henri Labrouste set himself to the task of designing the new *Bibliothèque Impériale* (later *Nationale*) in Paris. Already at the very start of the project, Labrouste had decided on an iron construction for its interior. That in itself was not an extraordinary choice, since from the mid-nineteenth century, iron had rapidly become widespread in the French construction industry, promoted for its affordability and incombustibility. His decision to keep the material visible and let the properties of iron guide his design does point to a specific awareness of the material. At the time, exposed iron constructions were restricted to infrastructural works and commercial buildings, and never visibly used in representational buildings for the state or cultural institutions. The material of choice for these projects had thus far been stone, whose properties had determined the architectural language for monumental buildings. Although classically trained at the Beaux-Arts and a state architect, Labrouste was somehow able to work his way past these conventions, letting iron determine the interior of an important national institute.[2] This essay explores in more detail the interaction between architect and material, using the case study of Labrouste to get a better understanding of the idea of material knowledge and its role in the design process.

Defining material knowledge

Before we turn to the Bibliothèque Nationale, we need to identify ideas of material knowing in the existing definitions of design knowledge. In an influential article from 1982, design theorist Nigel Cross describes 'designerly ways of knowing' as a form of embodied knowledge. In his definition of design, material knowledge is included as 'the collected experience of the material culture, and the collected body of experience, skill and understanding embodied in the arts of planning, inventing, making and doing'.[3] Cross understands material culture as a body of non-verbal codes, and every act of design as a manipulation of these codes. It is important to keep in mind that Cross's definition aimed to emancipate design thinking within academia, which was dominated by modes of thinking developed in the sciences and humanities. To demonstrate its value for the academic world, Cross described design as a form of conceptual problem-solving more than relating it to architectural practice or the sensorial experience of the built result. Certainly, buildings contain knowledge in their representation of cultural contexts, but they are also physical entities, manufactured at some point and composed of matter with specific properties. The building process itself is the moment when a design becomes a physical reality and where material understanding is crucial for a successful result.

Recent insights in other academic fields might be able to fill that lack of focus in Cross's definition and help to investigate the role of material knowledge. In the humanities, the so-called 'material turn' has put the role of materials centre stage, leading to new modes of thought.[4] Before, materials were seen as facilitators, 'afforders' at the most, but recent theories in these fields identify the character and agency of the material itself, acting in correspondence with the maker.[5] Art historian Ann-Sophie Lehmann also considers material knowledge in art as a dialogue between material and artist.[6] The study of the pedagogical ideas on material handling, developed by Bauhaus educator Moholy-Nagy, led her to coin the term 'material literacy', as 'a broad sensitivity to materials and their diverse meanings'.[7]

Relevant here is Lehmann's priority given to the idea of sensitivity.[8] Whereas Cross emphasizes the social and cultural knowledge residing in material objects, Lehmann stresses the importance of a sensorial or bodily relation to materials. She adds the adjective 'broad' with a double meaning and intent. For her, material literacy is a form of general knowledge, to be distinguished from the highly specific technical knowing and experience of, for example, the craftsman or the scientist. The 'broad' in her definition also refers to the responsibility of the designer to include a social (and environmental) awareness in their material handling. [9] A last remark concerns the combination of the words 'material' and 'literacy', stressing the dialogue between the maker's knowledge and the material properties, the artist depending on the materials and their modes of action.[10]

We can conclude that material knowledge in design and the arts forms a constellation of rational and tacit forms of knowledge. Combined with the scientific knowledge of material performance, this includes Cross's cultural notion of material and Lehmann's more skill- and sensitivity-based knowledge. In the next step, we return to the architect and the architectural project – the case of Labrouste's Bibliothèque Nationale – to see material knowledge in action.[11] How do the rational and more intuitive forms of material knowledge balance each other? How does the architect acquire this material knowledge? And lastly, how do materials inform and instigate the design project and shape the material knowing of the architect?

Material dialogues: Labrouste and iron

Henri Labrouste's first proposal for the Bibliothèque's reading room interior was not an act of genius but rather one of imitation (Fig. 1). He drew a domed room with a central rooflight, following the scheme of architect Smirke's recently completed London Library, with iron beams integrated into the ceiling, faintly visible but not in an outspoken way.[12] But at another point in the design, iron played a more prominent role. Apart from the reading room, a large archive space also had to be fitted into an existing courtyard, requiring an efficient use of space (Fig. 2). For these archives, Labrouste proposed a compact iron structure that cleverly included a bookcase system and contained slatted iron floors, enabling a maximized storage space of seven floors while allowing for light to enter deep into the building. The integrated application of iron demonstrated

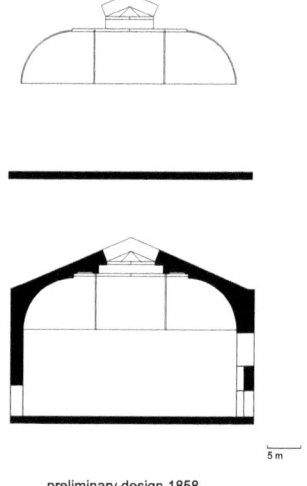

preliminary design 1858

Fig. 1. First design proposal, 1858: the reading room with single oculus and hidden iron beams (drawing Eireen Schreurs).

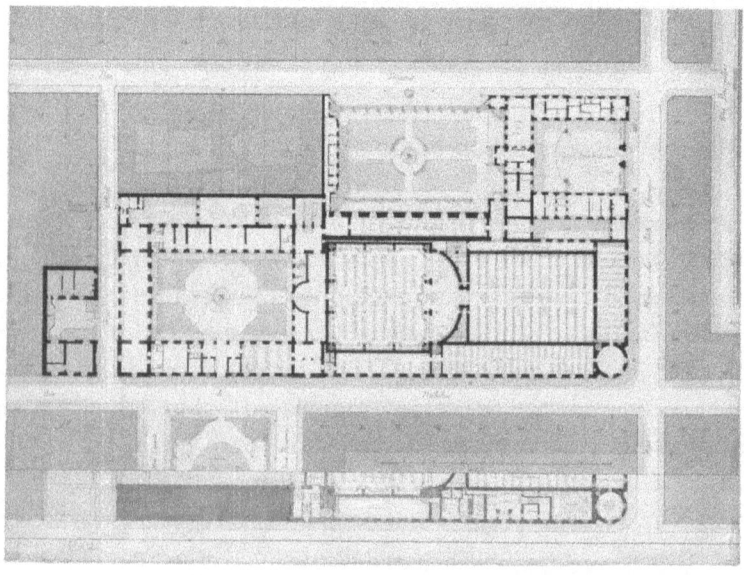

Fig. 2. Bibliothèque Impériale Plan d'Ensemble, 1869 (office Henri Labrouste).

Transformative Dialogues

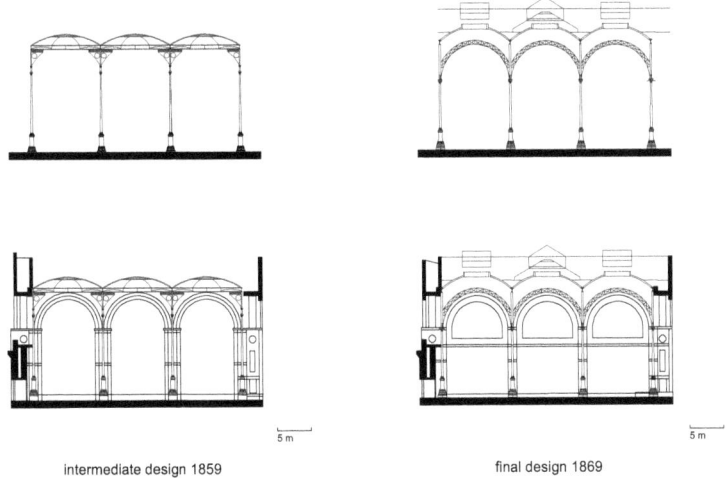

Fig. 3. Second design proposal, 1859: with flat roof and slightly bulging rooflights (drawing Eireen Schreurs).

Fig. 4. Reading room as executed with nine oculi and iron arches (drawing Eireen Schreurs).

Labrouste's technical understanding of the material, but the chosen solution also showed that Labrouste was able to visualize the atmospheric potential of the material. In Smirke's archive for the London Library, a similar structural system had been used, but here the archive space had been kept invisible for the visitors. Labrouste did exactly the opposite; in the design, he drew an enormous window linking the archive with the public reading room, putting the iron on full display, as an intricate Piranesian drawing.[13]

In the next design step, Labrouste returned to the structure of the reading room, reacting to the comments of colleague architect Felix Duban, who observed that the single rooflight of the dome could cause the readers' shadows to fall on their books. Labrouste changed the dome into a flat roof containing nine rooflights supported by a grid of iron beams (Fig. 3).[14] Labrouste placed iron columns under every knot of the grid, like a table with sixteen legs, with four freestanding columns, within the perimeter of a solid stone wall. The development of the roof marks a moment where the material enabled Labrouste to make a choice that would radically alter the character of the interior. Iron could have spanned the space in one go, but its compressive strength afforded the alternative of multiple columns that were so slender they almost disappeared.[15] The adage of Labrouste was that *'every material had to find its own form'*. The decision to put four columns in the middle of the room was an unprecedented move and a follow-up on his experiments with iron in an earlier project: the Bibliothèque Sainte Geneviève. It was Labrouste's recognition of iron's elegance that provided an alternative to the solid monumentality of the stone encasing of the room, even if it meant transgressing existing cultural conventions.

The reading room interior was now defined by the stark contrast of the massive stone walls to the slim iron construction. In consecutive steps, Labrouste worked to again soften this opposition by shaping the iron to mimic the stone, seeking resemblance in form and detailing. Labrouste changed the reading room roof a second time. He copied the arched forms of the perimeter stone wall to the iron structure, so that the iron roof bulged into nine cupolas (Fig. 4). Also, in the ornamentation of the pedestals, the iron columns started to bear a strong formal resemblance to their stone counterparts. This might seem strange, but not so much if you understand the realities of construction in those days. The process of casting required a wooden mould that was chiselled by the *artisan-sculpteur* Perrin, the same craftsman who executed some of the stone- and woodwork of the reading room interior.[16] Did Labrouste's 'to every material its own form' not apply to the detailing? Did his material knowledge end here, having the craftsman taking over? It is more complicated than that. The iron columns were classical in form and detail, but Labrouste must have been aware of their surreal appearance: the shafts were uncannily thin and the tiny Corinthian capitals almost seemed to ridicule the classical stone orders. The profiles of the iron pedestals were just a bit sharper, bending slightly downward, as if Labrouste wanted to acknowledge iron's liquid character.[17] The details show a play with the cultural codes and suggest that his search for a proper representation of iron was aided by an artisanal understanding of the processes of making. The reconciliation of iron's radically different character with the classical canon was also enabled by Labrouste's personal style, characterized by elegance and refinement, which was recognizable in all his architectural work, up to his handwriting and the miniature sketches in his many black notebooks.

How architects sense materials

What the design process of the Bibliothèque reveals is that varied forms of material knowing were in operation within every step of the design. But what also becomes apparent is how, at crucial moments, Labrouste's intuitive sensitivity for the material enabled him to steer the project away from conventional solutions towards innovation and the creation of new experiences. This calls to mind the distinction posed by philosopher Gilbert Ryle between 'knowing that and knowing how'; technical and cultural knowledge do not suffice to act, rather an architect can only make knowledge productive through a more intuitive 'knowing how'. This does raise the question of how architects are able to acquire this material sensitivity. Unlike the craftsman or artist, the architect never handles the material himself and, as a consequence, lacks the experience of its resistance. It is true that architects make decisions when the project is only on paper. At some point, however, any designer faces the consequences of his design in the reality of the project. This renders material experience into a process of continuous evaluation, a feedback loop, allowing the designer to test issues such as scale, proportion, textures, material combinations, etc. over the course of several projects. Apparently, this material experience can be *imagined*, the architect building upon existing knowledge and experience. This is why in the Bauhaus *Materialkurz*, Moholy-Nagy included *handwerk*. It not only trained the senses, such as vision, sound and tactility but also sharpened the technique of imagining.

Labrouste could visualize the material reality of the iron construction in his archive, seeing it so vividly that he imagined a large window to go with it, at a moment when the design was only a first idea. His visit to Smirke's archive with the attractive filigree structure, dramatically skylit, must have made a lasting impression, enabling him to mentally transplant this idea to his own building. The sketchbook of his visit to London does not contain sketches of Smirke's reading room; it only shows precise details of the archive structure, demonstrating that he recognized the potential of iron straight away, waiting for a fit moment to apply it. Indeed, Labrouste probably never processed iron himself, but he must have seen others doing so, often. Labrouste instructed the mould maker of the iron columns, paying visits to the atelier. And for the duration of the construction, a temporary office-annexe was located right next to the construction site, giving him the sounds, smells and slow progress of the building as a multi-sensorial feedback.

And Labrouste used the tool of drawing. According to anthropologist Tim Ingold, in drawing, you can become the object that you draw. It is a tool for sensitizing, the drawing tracing the object as 'an archive of its maker's muscles'.[18] The draughtsman can reach a certain form of direct experience by rebuilding the design with the eye. As a *Prix de Rome* laureate, Labrouste had spent an impressive five years in Italy redrawing the buildings from the Roman times and the Renaissance, which had made him an outstanding draughtsman. His drawings of the period can be interpreted as detailed investigations into various materials, for which he applied different techniques. The more atmospheric sketches and watercolour drawings allowed him to 'feel' the material and trace its textures, irregularities, treatment and weathering. The architectural, measured drawings offered him the possibility to understand materials from their structural logic and build-up.[19] Later, Labrouste also filled many sketchbooks, revealing a continuous recording and testing of ideas in very delicate drawings, the books often not larger than a business card.

Fig 5. Interior of the *Salle de Travail* or reading room at the inauguration, as published in *Le Monde*, 1868 (drawing B.Y. Linton).

How materials innovate

So then, lastly, what is the role of the material itself in the production of material knowledge? The TACK network is founded on the idea that tacit knowledge holds the specific capacity to respond to change.[20] In the case of material knowing, we have seen that material change instigates a design response; it arouses the interest of the designer and tickles the imagination. In his book *The Craftsman*, Richard Sennett describes how the craftsman is aware of material forces through his or her 'material consciousness'.[21] This consciousness is sharpened by the 'alchemical translation of materials into architecture'. That Semper was equally fascinated by material change and its potential to innovate can be inferred from his idea of *Stoffwechsel*, a phenomenon whereby existing forms are renewed through the introduction of new materials.[22]

How this process of material change operates in the design process can be seen if we return to Labrouste once more. The dialogue between stone and iron became the prime generator of the reading room, allowing Labrouste to use the codes of stone as providers of meaning while at the same time transforming them. The material reality of iron allowed Labrouste to dismantle the premises on which classical architecture was built. The dialogue between the wall and the iron structure that had started from a constructional logic also fuelled its detailing. Labrouste proposed an architecture of light and refinement, dramatizing the contrast between the different origins of the materials: the earthy, massive materiality of the stone versus the fluid formlessness of iron. In doing so, the iron column bases could start to be read as iron weights, keeping the elegant roof structure from flying away. (Fig. 5) Out of an innovative sensitivity to the properties of iron, a dematerialized architecture arose, predicting what would become a prime concern of modern architecture.[23]

To close

This article is a first dig into the idea of material knowing, revealing how material sensitivity operates as a decisive driving force in the creative process. The moment an architectural idea has to be transformed into a physical construct, the material sensitivity brings scales, materials and spatial effects together, laying relations, opposing, reconciliating or simply creating aesthetic delight. Sensitivity is also a dominant mode of thinking in moments when the design starts to operate beyond material conventions, beyond facts and technical constraints, forcing the creation of something that did not exist before: a material culture yet unknown. Architects acquire this aspect of material knowing through a personal preference for certain materials, which can be traced back to their biography and earlier work, ultimately resulting in an oeuvre where ideological, stylistic and material preferences merge. Is it a coincidence that the refinement of Labrouste's handwriting and drawing is also visible in his architectural style and that this quest for elegance bound him for life to the material that could provide him with the means to create it?

The unique conditions of architecture, as a social, cultural, political and aesthetic project, feed the creative knowing of the architect, who seeks to translate these conditions into a form and material that are meaningful or even create new meanings. With the Bibliothèque, Labrouste constructed both an intimate and transparent palace for knowledge. In order to open the building up to all who sought knowledge, he used a construction that was associated with more mundane programmes, lowering the library's threshold while creating optimal reading conditions.[24] Material knowledge concentrates the overwhelming complexity of the assignment into a simple column in the centre of the room and with this single gesture, gives iron a new form and future.

Notes

1 'Labrouste, le premier, comprit tout le parti que l'on pouvait tirer de l'emploi du fer, non comme une ossature à cacher sous les formes anciennes, mais comme un nouveau moyen de construction devant rester franchement accusé par des formes nouvelles.' M. Lapine was an architect and chef of the historical monuments department. *Souvenirs d'Henri Labrouste, architecte, membre d'institute: notes recueillies et classées par ses enfants et ses élèves* (Fontainebleau: Cuénot, 1928), 67.
2 Bertrand Lemoine, 'Labrouste and Iron', in: Corinne Belier, Barry Bergdoll and Marc Le Coeur (eds.), *Henri Labrouste: Structure Brought to Light* (New York: The Museum of Modern Art, New York, 2013), 181.
3 Nigel Cross, 'Designerly Ways of Knowing', *Design Issues* 3:4 (October 1982), 221.
4 As Tim Ingold and Jane Bennett (amongst others) have remarked, the hylomorphic model, or the primacy of idea over matter, has been the dominant mode of thinking throughout modernity. Jane Bennett, *Vibrant Matter, A Political Ecology of Things* (Durham: Duke University Press, 2010), 56.

5   Ann-Sophie Lehmann, 'The Matter of the Medium. Some Tools for an Art Theoretical Interpretation of Materials', in: Christy Anderson, Anne Dunlop and Pamela H. Smith (eds.), *The Matter of Art: Materials, Technologies, Meanings 1200–1700* (Manchester: Manchester University Press, 2015), 21–41.

6   Lehmann, 'The Matter of the Medium'.

7   Ann-Sophie Lehmann, 'Material Literacy', *Zeitschrift Bauhaus* 9 (2017), 20–27.

8   Laszlo Moholy-Nagy, *The New Vision 1928 and Abstract of an Artist* (New York: Wittenborn Schultz Inc., 1947), 17.

9   Literacy is, according to the Oxford dictionary: 1. To read and write 2. Having education or knowledge typically in a specified area. Nigel Cross describes designers as 'having the ability to both read and write: they understand what messages objects communicate, and they can create new objects which embody new messages'. Cross, 'Designerly Ways of Knowing', 225.

10 The term 'literate' translates into German as 'gebildet', a term that translates itself back again as 'educated'.

11 The Labrouste archives on the building are extensive (700 pieces) but by no means complete. This article is based on an initial study of the archives at the Bibliothèque Nationale de France (BnF) and the Labrouste sketchbooks at the Académie d'Architecture, in 2019 and 2020.

12 Many buildings at the time in Paris had hidden iron ceiling structures, though cupolas were rare. One famous and much older example is the Halles aux Blés (1811), which was covered with an iron roof containing an oculus.

13 Henri's brother and colleague Theodore had copied the work of Piranesi, stripping it of its baroque details, putting more emphasis on structure and light. Francisco Javier Girón Sierra, 'Understanding Roman Construction Before A. Choisy: Piranesi and his Influence on Rondelet', in: James W.P. Campbell et al., *Studies in the History of Construction, Second Conference of the Construction History Society* (Cambridge: Construction History Society, 2015), 11–21. Labrouste's alternative, more radical option contained even vaster glass panels between the archive and reading room. Neil Levine, 'Paths Not Taken: Little-known Projects by Henri Labrouste for the Bibliothèque Nationale' (conference BNF Richelieu 'Un projet en question', Institut National d'Histoire de l'Art, 5–6 July 2010).

14 The section described here resembles the final design, but the flat ceiling, the absence of the iron cupolas and the iron triangular stability angles demonstrate that this is an earlier version, not described in the existing literature.

15 Freestanding columns did not make a first appearance in this project. His earlier Ste Geneviève Library had iron columns as well, but they stood in a row, as in train stations of the time. The non-directional grid of the proposal not only avoided an association with infrastructural works but also introduced a more informal non-hierarchy in the reading room. David van Zanten, 'Marble's Translucence and What Mid-nineteenth Century Architects Made of It', symposium 'Marble', Florence, 2010.

16 There are different sources for the name of the sculptor. Pierre Saddy mentions Lorrain, but without providing a source. The *Archive Nationale* file F21/2915A mentions a payment on 31.05.64 to Auguste Perrin for making the models for the columns. In F21/2915B the same Perrin was paid for wooden and stone ornaments.

17 Labrouste sketched the iron and stone columns next to each other, ending in profiles that were much more alike than in the beginning. From the school textbook of Pierre Chabat, *Fragments d'Architecture; Egypte, Grèce, Rome, Moyen age; Renaissance, age moderne, etc; avec notices descriptives* (Paris: Morel, 1868), plate 56. That the difference between iron and stone detailing was considered relevant in his time is demonstrated by the fact that the iron and stone pedestals were printed next to each other.

18   James Elkins, quoted in Tim Ingold, 'The Textility of Making', *Cambridge Journal of Economics* 34:1 (2010), 99.

19   Labrouste caused quite a scandal with his infamous Paestum drawings, of which the argument for an alternative dating of the Paestum temples was based on a precise observation of the buildings as material objects. Martin Bressani, 'The Paestum Controversy', in: Corinne Beliel, Barry Bergdoll and Marc Le Coeur (eds.), *Henri Labrouste, Structure Brought to Light* (New York: The Museum of Modern Art, 2013), 88–93.

20   ERC-funded training network 'Communities of Tacit Knowledge: Architecture and its Ways of Knowing' (2019–2023, project no. 860413).

21   Richard Sennett, *The Craftsman*, (London: Penguin Books, 2008), 120–144.

22   Akos Moravánszky, *Metamorphism, Material Change in Architecture* (Basel: Birkhäuser, 2017), 15.

23   That this was by no means self-evident, becomes clear when Semper writes in 'Style' that it is not possible to speak of monumental iron or cast-iron style for 'their ideal is invisible architecture'. Moravánszky, *Metamorphism,* 242.

24   The reading room was public but not for everyone. The library had a problem of homeless people seeking shelter before the refurbishment and, therefore, Labrouste created a *salle de lecture* for the general public in the old building, while the *salle de travail* was reserved for accredited researchers. Corinne Beliel, Barry Bergdoll and Marc Le Coeur, (eds.), *Henri Labrouste, Structure Brought to Light* (New York: Museum of Modern Art, New York, 2013), 176.

Bibliography

Beliel, Corinne, Barry Bergdoll and Marc Le Coeur (eds.), *Henri Labrouste: Structure Brought to Light* (New York: Museum of Modern Art, New York, 2013)

Bennett, Jane, *Vibrant Matter, A Political Ecology of Things* (Durham: Duke University Press, 2010)

Bressani, Martin, 'The Paestum Controversy', in: Corinne Beliel, Barry Bergdoll and Marc Le Coeur (eds.), *Henri Labrouste, Structure Brought to Light* (New York: The Museum of Modern Art, 2013), 88–93

Chabat, Pierre, *Fragments d'Architecture; Egypte, Grèce, Rome, Moyen Age; Renaissance, Age Moderne, etc; Avec Notices Descriptives* (Paris: Morel, 1868)

Cross, Nigel, 'Designerly Ways of Knowing', *Design Issues* 3:4 (October 1982), 221–227

Girón Sierra, Francisco Javier, 'Understanding Roman Construction before A. Choisy: Piranesi and his Influence on Rondelet', in: James W.P. Campbell et al., *Studies in the History of Construction, Second Conference of the Construction History Society* (Cambridge: Construction History Society, 2015), 11–21

Ingold, Tim, 'The Textility of Making', *Cambridge Journal of Economics* 34:1 (2010), 91–102

Labrouste, Henri, Labrouste archive, files F21/2915A, F21/2915B, *Archives Nationales de France*, Bibliothèque Nationale de France

Lehmann, Ann-Sophie, 'The Matter of the Medium. Some Tools for an Art Theoretical Interpretation of Materials', in: Christy Anderson, Anne Dunlop, and Pamela H. Smith (eds.), *The Matter of Art: Materials, Technologies, Meanings 1200–1700* (Manchester: Manchester University Press, 2015), 21–41

Lehmann, Ann-Sophie, 'Material Literacy' *Zeitschrift Bauhaus* 9 (2017), 20–27

Lemoine, Bertrand, 'Labrouste and Iron', in: Corinne Belier, Barry Bergdoll and Marc Le Coeur (eds.), *Henri Labrouste: Structure Brought to Light* (New York: The Museum of Modern Art, New York, 2013), 181–191

Levine, Neil, 'Paths Not Taken: Little-known Projects by Henri Labrouste for the Bibliothèque Nationale', Conference BNF Richelieu 'Un Projet en Question', Institut National d'Histoire de l'Art, 5–6 July 2010

Moholy-Nagy, Laszlo, *The New Vision 1928 and Abstract of an Artist* (New York: Wittenborn, Schultz, Inc., 1947)

Moravánszky, Akos, *Metamorphism, Material Change in Architecture* (Basel: Birkhäuser, 2017)

Sennett, Richard, *The Craftsman* (London: Penguin Books, 2008)

Souvenirs d'Henri Labrouste, Architecte, Membre d'Institute: Notes Recueillies et Classées par ses Enfants et ses Élèves (Fontainebleau: Cuénot, 1928)

Van Zanten, David, 'Marble's Translucence and What Mid-nineteenth Century Architects Made of It', Symposium 'Marble', Florence, 2010

A Black Box? Architecture and its Epistemes

Tom Avermaete

It was probably the British critic Reyner Banham who most adequately qualified the general status of architectural knowledge, when he wrote in his posthumously published essay 'A Black Box: The Secret Profession of Architecture': 'I propose to treat the architectural mode or presence as a classic 'black box', recognized by its output though unknown in its contents'.[1] Banham correctly identified that architectural artefacts, our buildings and cities, are intensively discussed and criticized but that the underpinning design knowledge is hardly ever scrutinized. He questioned in his essay what 'architects uniquely do' and applauded attempts as Christopher Alexander's pattern language, as an 'approximate description of what architects actually do when they do architecture'.[2]

Banham's essay was an attempt to identify the value of the knowledge that is generated in the very act of architectural design, but he simultaneously criticized how architecture distanced itself from all other knowledge fields in society because of its closed and obscure character. The English critic lamented how architects increasingly distinguished themselves from other professional groups in society, by keeping the basis and logics of their profession secret. Retrospectively, Banham's essay reads as a populist critique that urged the opening up of the field of architectural design, so as to initiate more exchange with society.

However, Banham's essay also prompts a different consideration; it invites us to reflect upon the content of the 'black box'. It prompts us to contemplate the character, the *modus operandi* and the role of architectural design knowledge. This is not an easy task. First, this is because – as Banham rightly noted – architects have intentionally kept the knowledge base of their profession vague and secret, often in an attempt to discriminate the profession of architecture from other professions such as that of the engineer. Second, architecture knowledge seems difficult to unravel because it is articulated through a unique entanglement of tools, processes and things.

Beyond innocence: the existence of epistemes

In this essay, I want to pay special attention to one of the initial moments in the design process: the analysis of the territorial or urban condition in which the architect will be intervening. Though many architects maintain that this is an exploratory and open phase in the design process, I would argue that the contrary is true. This analysis, that it is just any other moment in the design process, is all but innocent. Specific 'frames of value and thought' drive the logos and praxis of the architect during the initial analysis. Sometimes these thought frames are very explicit and articulated loudly in texts. At other times, they remain completely silent and hidden. The French philosopher Michel Foucault has called these thought frames 'epistemes'. He writes:

> I would define the episteme retrospectively as the strategic apparatus [...] The episteme is the 'apparatus' which makes possible the separation, not of the true from the false, but of what may from what may not be characterized as scientific.[3]

While Foucault was writing about science, it is possible to draw parallels with our own field. In architecture too, we can discover several of these epistemes that act as comprehensive frameworks for the analysis, understanding and conception of the built environment. Specific to architectural culture is that these epistemes are not consecutive or mutually exclusive. In other words, in architecture there is never a single dominant episteme. Quite the contrary. As the English critic Charles Jencks illustrates in his famous chart of the developments of twentieth-century architecture, in our field, several epistemes seem to function at once. In architectural culture, epistemes are simultaneous and complementary.

A Black Box? 71

Time and time again, these epistemes are activated by designers in the analysis of the existing built environment, as well as for the design of new buildings and neighbourhoods. However, very often this activation is not explicitly reflected upon. Most often, epistemes remain tacit in architectural culture; they are considered as recognized, self-evident, or – in some cases – even as 'given' or 'engrained' in the built environment. This essay is an attempt to uncover some of these epistemes. It is an attempt to lift the lid of the 'black box' and raise awareness about some of the epistemes that have been around for a long time in architecture culture and have informed architectural thinking and practice in the past two centuries.

ty·pol·ogy (tī päl'ə jē): noun. the study of types[4]

A first episteme that we can discover in architectural culture can be qualified as typology and relates to the study of types. In general terms, a *type* is usually understood as sharing characteristics with other people or things, and as such, forming an identifiable group within a larger set. In architecture, the idea of type has its own particular history and has played a substantial role in the understanding of the built environment.[5]

The nineteenth-century French architect and educator Jean-Nicolas-Louis Durand was one of the first to conceive of the built environment in this specific way. In his renowned publication *Recueil et parallèle des édifices de tout genre anciens et modernes* of 1801, Durand illustrates what such an episteme could offer for the understanding of the built environment.[6] One of his examples is churches from various time periods. Across geographies and scales, as well as material and stylistic differences, Durand illustrates that different churches can be understood as belonging to the same group of occurrences in the built environment (Fig. 1). For Durand, particular modern and Gothic churches belong to the same typology because they share characteristics of spatial disposition: the tripartite division, the axiality and the symmetry of the church.

In Durand's view, type is defined as a combination of static and dynamic elements. While some of the main characteristics of the spatial disposition remain static, the materiality, style and size of the churches differ. The static parameters make a building part of a typological group.

Durand uses the architectural type both in diachronic and synchronic comparative studies. In other words, type allows Durand to see relationships between buildings that have been realized in different eras, but it also offers him the opportunity to make connections between different buildings that are simultaneously realized.

One of the most important characteristics of this typological approach to the built environment is that it focuses on built form. The tools of the architect are adjusted to this particular perspective. Hence, in the approach of Durand, the ground plan, cross-section and façade drawing – all understood as precise descriptions of built architectural form – play a paramount role. In Durand's *Recueil et Parallèle des Édifices de Tout Genre*, precise plans, sections and façades of different buildings are juxtaposed. Together, they constitute the evidence for the existence of certain types within the built environment.

When Jean-Nicolas-Louis Durand was no longer analysing but instead designing new buildings, he acted within the same episteme. In his lectures for students at the Ecole Polytechnique in Paris, published as *Précis* in 1802, the design of a new museum does not start from a programmatic

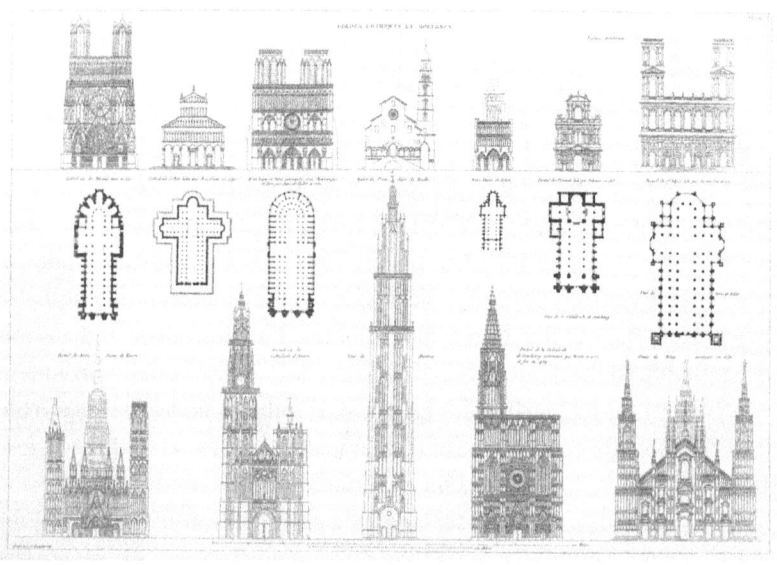

Fig. 1. Gothic and modern churches. From Jean-Nicolas-Louis Durand, *Recueil et Parallèle des Édifices de Tout Genre Anciens et Modernes*, 1801.

analysis but rather from an ideal typological proposal.[7] In other words, for Durand, architectural design is understood as the development of variations on a type. It should come as no surprise that the tools that informed the architectural analysis reappear. Indeed, we see again that the ground plan, cross-section and façade drawing are for Durand the main tools of architectural action, both analytical and projective.

Typology was not only an episteme of the nineteenth century but also gained great importance in the twentieth century. Around 1960, the lens of typology reappeared in the Italian architectural and urban debate on typo-morphology.[8] A group of Italian architects reacted against the hypothesis of international style modernism, and made a plea to reconsider the principles and rationales of the historical urban tissue.

It was the Italian architect and urban planner Saverio Muratori who reinvented the episteme of typology in his *Studi Per Una Operante Storia Urbana Di Venezia* in 1959.[9] In this comprehensive historical analysis of the city of Venice, Muratori investigates the evolution of the city through a very precise description of the built form of neighbourhoods and buildings. Using the instrument of the ground plan drawing, he illustrates how buildings and neighbourhoods have had the capacity to accommodate change throughout time, while maintaining some of their formal and spatial characteristics. For Muratori, the city is a material organism that changes and adapts constantly. His drawings illustrate, for instance, how the inner partitions of houses have transformed through the centuries to comply with changing dwelling patterns, while maintaining their outer presence and thus their formal and visual relation to the city. This led Muratori to the conclusion that there exists a type of the Venice house, which remains stable in terms of urban form (morphology) while offering the opportunity for change in its architecture (typology).

When Muratori moves to the realm of design, he works within the same episteme. His design for the neighbourhood Barene di San Giuliano (1959), a new project for the city of Venice, is not based on functional zoning, as would have been the case in a modernist plan, but rather on the clear description of the typology of urban perimeter blocks and the resulting morphology of the neighbourhood. Typology and morphology are pronounced with the tool of the ground plan drawing, which defines with great precision the intended built form. Other Italian architects such as Aldo Rossi and Carlo Aymonino worked in the same episteme from the beginning of the 1960s, just as the French school of Versailles, with Panerai and Castex, would work in the footsteps of Muratori from the 1980s onwards.[10]

phe·nom·enol·ogy (fə näm'ə näl'ə jē) noun. the philosophical study of phenomena, specif., such a study of perceptual experience[11]

A second episteme that has dominated architectural thinking and practice in the nineteenth and twentieth centuries is phenomenology. Indeed, architecture and the city have long been addressed as phenomena that are mainly about perception and experience. An early example of this episteme is to be found in the *Histoire de l'Architecture* (1899) by French historian Auguste Choisy.[12] In his study, Choisy analyses the Acropolis in Athens. However, this is not done from a morpho-typological viewpoint – precisely describing the built form of the Acropolis – but rather from the multiple perspectives from which the Acropolis is experienced (Fig. 2).

In contrast to Durand, the interest of Choisy is not so much the precise and actual built form, but rather the various ways in which the site and the buildings of the Acropolis are perceived by its visitors. This is clearly reflected in the tools that are employed. In a combination of movement diagrams (composed of a schematic plan with numbers indicating the different vantage points) and perspective drawings of the different built structures, Choisy attempts to convey the sequence of experiences of the visitor while gradually moving on the Acropolis. For Choisy, who was a professor at the *École des Ponts et Chaussées* in Paris, architecture is first and foremost a landscape of perception.[13]

In the twentieth century, the critical capacity of the episteme of phenomenology would be activated by the British architect Gordon Cullen in his well-known book *The Concise Townscape* (1961).[14] In this publication, he offered a critique of the rational and open model of modernist urban planning, but also made a strong plea to recuperate the urban experience of the historical city. In his attempt to describe the lost qualities of the historical city, Cullen did not choose a typo-morphological investigation, but rather a so-called 'serial vision' that combined the subsequent visual impressions of a pedestrian walking through a medieval city. In order

A Black Box?

to transmit these various phenomena, *The Concise Townscape* employs specific tools; it combines a series of perspectives illustrating the subsequent views with a diagrammatic plan that illustrates the followed path. Together, the perspectives and plan depict the qualities of the town as a matter of movement and altering perception.

The American architect and urban designer Kevin Lynch chose the episteme of phenomenology to criticize the dense and unstructured character of the contemporary city. In his seminal publication *The Image of the City* (1960), Lynch maintained that an analysis of the urban condition should start from so-called 'mental maps'.[15] These maps were based on interviews that probed the perception and mental representation of the urban environment by citizens. Lynch held that these mental representations were defined by perceptual anchor points in the city: paths, edges, districts, nodes and landmarks. As a tool, Lynch used a combination of schematic maps with photography in order to capture the perception and mental mapping of citizens. Consequently, Lynch defined design

Fig. 2. Movement diagram and perspective of the Acropolis in Athens. From Auguste Choisy, *Histoire de l'Architecture*, 1899.

as intervening in the mental maps of citizens. In his view, the designer should work on paths, edges, districts, nodes and landmarks to make the city more legible.

se·mi·ol·o·gy (sē'mē-ŏl'ə-jē) noun. the study of signs[16]

A third important episteme that is at work in the field of architecture is semiology. Approaching the built environment as a collection of signs that can be deciphered or even 'read' as a language is one of the epistemes that was rather short lived. Among the most explicit proponents of this episteme are Venturi and Scott Brown, in their study *Learning from Las Vegas* (1972).[17] In their seminal analysis of Las Vegas, Venturi and Scott Brown do not read the urban condition as built form, nor as a perceptual landscape, but rather as an assembly of signs (Fig. 3). Their instruments are adjusted to this particular episteme. Venturi and Scott Brown use

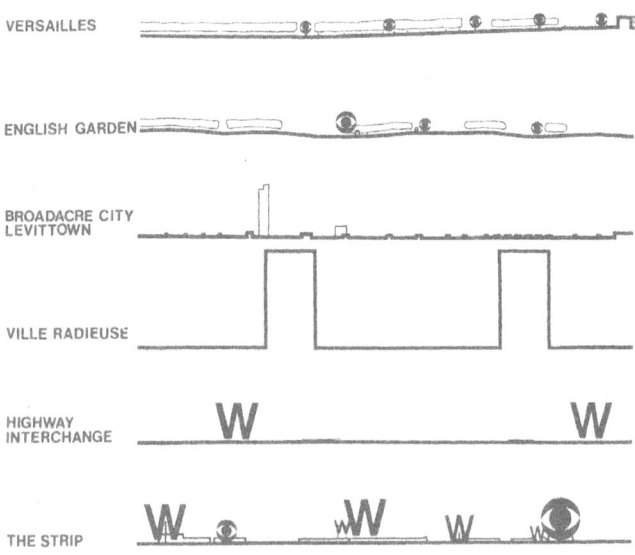

Fig. 3. 'Space, Scale, Speed, Symbol: A Comprehensive Analysis of Vast Spaces'. From Robert Venturi, Denise Scott Brown and Steven Izenour, *Learning from Las Vegas: The Forgotten Symbolism of Architectural Form*, 1972.

diagrams to investigate the urban condition of Las Vegas from this semiological perspective. The well-known distinction between a 'duck' and 'decorated shed' is a prime example of this approach, but their 'Speed-Scale-Symbol' diagrams also illustrate how they maintain that changing mobility requires changing signs in the urban territory.

In 1970, Venturi and Scott Brown used a similar method to investigate the standardized company settlement of Levittown. This housing estate was planned, built and sold by a single developer, the company of Abraham Levitt and Sons. The Levitts devised a mass-production scheme that allowed them to build inexpensive housing for the post-war flood of veterans and their families. Levittown was characterized by uniformity but also by many small and large interventions by inhabitants. In their investigation 'Learning from Levittown', Venturi and Scott Brown analyse the built environment through the use of symbolic decorative attachments, the wagon wheels, post and rail ranch fences, coach lights and flagpoles that were becoming the standard appliqué of middle-class American homes.[18]

The analysis used very specific instruments and focused on the changes that owners had made: 'how they have decorated them on the outside and dealt with their lawns in individual ways'.[19] In large collages, Venturi and Scott Brown confront drawings and photographs of these signs of the middle class with the way in which houses were represented in television commercials, home journals, car advertisements, cartoons, films and even soap operas. As Scott Brown puts it, they did 'lots of content analysis looking at what we called literature, but the literature was Disney cartoons on Daisy Duck, sitcoms, ads on television, articles in *Popular Mechanics* magazine or builders' journals'. In this comparative fashion, they are able to illustrate the symbolic charge of the different signs that people are adding to their homes. In the designs for buildings and neighbourhoods by Venturi and Scott Brown, signs – both popular and disciplinary – would get a paramount place. They were a means to situate their buildings and cities both in the world of users and of architects.

Praxeology (prak-sē-ä-lə-jē) noun. the study of human action and conduct

In the field of architecture, there exists a long tradition of approaching the built environment through the ways that it is practised. In this episteme, the manifold practices of dwelling and building are at the centre of attention. Bruno Taut's, *Die neue Wohnung – Die Frau als Schöpferin* (1924) is a good example of such an episteme.[20] In this book, we find reprints of the study 'Steps Taken in the Preparation of a Meal' by the English household specialist Christine Frederick. Through diagrams and schemes, Taut visualizes how the kitchen in the house is used to prepare a meal. The built environment does not appear here as a material reality, nor as a series of signs, but rather as an abstracted stage for everyday practices. Taut studied spatial practices in function of their rationalization. Taylorization and ergonomics offered an important intellectual base for his investigations. Similar approaches to the built environment can be found in Margarete Schütte-Lihotzky's design for the Frankfurter Küche (1926) and in the work of Ernst Neufert for his so-called *Architect's Data* (1936).

Within the same episteme, but from another intellectual perspective, are a set of studies that appeared in the ninth *Congrès International d'Architecture Moderne* (CIAM) in 1953.[21] This main platform of the modern movement in architecture presented a set of studies that looked into spatial practices in the built environment from their 'socio-spatial' character. CIAM architects normally used a system that Le Corbusier had introduced in 1946 as the CIAM Grid or *Grille*: a large matrix composed according to fixed CIAM categories that allowed for the presentation of an avant-garde urban project in a standard fashion. They believed that the Grid was one of the tools by which different modern design solutions could be compared and thus would offer the basis for finding universal solutions for the future city. However, instead of showing a hyper-modern design for a new urban neighbourhood – as was normally done in CIAM Grids – two North African groups at the ninth CIAM in 1953 focused on a completely different urban environment: the *bidonville*, or shantytown (Fig. 4).

The group GAMMA (*Groupe d'Architectes Modernes Marocains*), led by the French urban planner Michel Ecochard and the architect Georges Candilis, represented investigations of the Carrières Centrales *bidonville* in the Moroccan city of Casablanca. It was composed of a large series of sketches, photographs and collages that documented the living conditions in the *bidonville* in both the private and collective spheres. Another group of North African architects, the CIAM-Alger group under the leadership of architects such as Roland Simounet and Michel Emery, presented the Bidonville Mahieddine Grid.[22] The grid for the shantytown of Mahieddine, on the outskirts of Algiers, showed a very detailed study of the reasons for the emergence of the *bidonville* – the sanitary and health problems that it brought to the fore, photographic and graphic analyses of the way that the *bidonville* was practised, as well as design proposals for new housing units that were to replace the shantytown.

To investigate the *bidonville*, the young French architects relied upon a tradition of anthropological research developed at the *Service de l'Urbanisme* in Casablanca, Morocco. After the Second World War, this urban services department of the French protectorate initiated large programmes for the investigation of indigenous dwelling patterns in towns and villages. To their credit, the French architects did not confine this methodology to the terrain of traditional rural environments. The everyday urban spaces of the *bidonvilles* of Casablanca or Algiers were investigated in a similar ethnological fashion, through tracings and photographs. By using

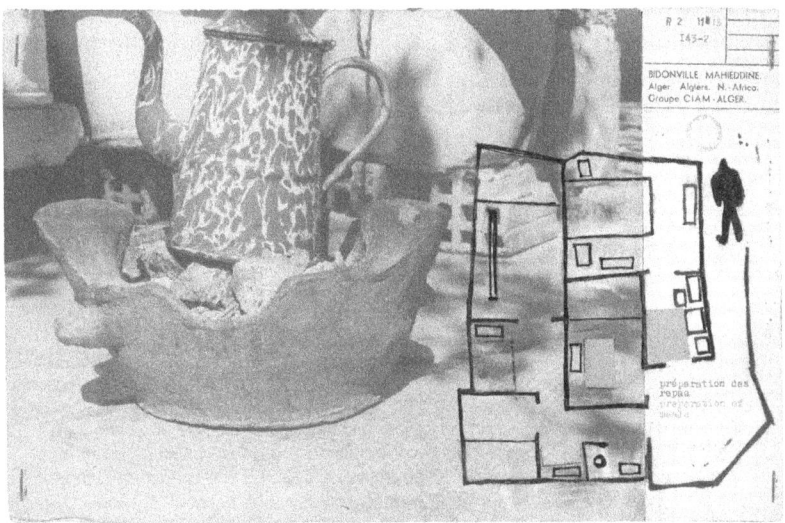

Fig. 4. Investigation of the *bidonville*. From CIAM-Alger group, *Bidonville Mahieddine Grid*, CIAM 9, Aix-en-Provence, 1953.

this approach, the architects of GAMMA and CIAM-Alger were able to depict the *bidonville* as the substance of daily practices of dwelling and building, as the material through which inhabitants leave the most rudimentary symbolic and spatial traces in the built environment. The *bidonville* was described as the locus of symbolic and spatial struggles. In the North African CIAM Grids, spatial practices are considered as conscious, and thus meaningful, spatial expressions. They are the articulations of negotiations and re-negotiations between conscious and active subjects.

In conclusion

Architectural culture works along a large variety of epistemes, of which I only present four. Nevertheless, this small overview illustrates that epistemes are at work in the field of architecture. They are related to a specific set of tools – ranging from drawing to collage and diagram – and methods, including mapping, charting and fieldwork. Epistemes are the bridges between investigation and projection, between analysis and design. They are specific thought frames from which architects operate and that provide a basis for analysis, comprehension and intervention in the built environment. Epistemes – sometimes a single one but most often a combination of many – offer a horizon for the delineation, formulation and composition of architectural projects.

Notes

1. Mary Banham et al. (eds.), *A Critic Writes. Selected Essays by Reyner Banham* (Los Angeles: University of California Press, 1996), XX.
2. Mary Banham et al. (eds.), *A Critic Writes*, XX.
3. Michel Foucault, Colin Gordon, *Power/Knowledge: Selected Interviews and Other Writings, 1972-1977* (New York: Pantheon Books, 1980), 197.
4. *Webster's New World College Dictionary*.
5. General introductions to the notions of type and typology in the field of architecture can be found in Alan Colquhoun, 'Modern Architecture and the Symbolic Dimension of the Type and its Transformation', in: Alan Colquhoun, *Essays in Architectural Criticism; Modern Architecture and Historical Change* (Cambridge, MA; London: MIT Press, 1989), 43–50; Rob Krier, 'Typological and Morphological Elements of the Concept of Space', in: Rob Krier, *Urban Space* (London: Academy Editions, 1988), 22–61; Rafael Moneo, 'On Typology', *Oppositions* 13 (Summer, 1978), 23–44; Anthony Vidler, 'The Third Typology', *Oppositions* 7 (1976), 1–4.

6 Jean-Nicolas-Louis Durand, *Recueil et Parallèle des Édifices de Tout Genre, Anciens et Modernes* (Paris: Chez l'auteur, à l'école Polytechnique, 1801).

7 Jean-Nicolas-Louis Durand, *Précis Des Leçons d'Architecture Données à l'École Royale Polytechnique* (Paris: Durand, 1802).

8 For the Italian conceptions of typology see, for instance: Giulio Carlo Argan, 'On the Typology of Architecture', *Architectural Design* (December 1963), 564–565; Aldo Rossi, 'Problems of Classification', *The Architecture of the City* (Cambridge, MA; London: MIT Press, 1992 [orig. 1966]), 48–54.

9 Saverio Muratori, *Studi Per Una Operante Storia Urbana Di Venezia* (Roma: Istituto Poligrafico dello Stato, 1960). An introduction to Muratori and typology can be found in Giancarlo Cataldi, Gian Luigi Maffei and Paola Vaccaro, 'Saverio Muratori and the Italian School of Planning Typology', *Urban Morphology* 6:1 (2002), 3–14.

10 Philippe Panerai, Jean Castex and Jean-Charles Depaule, *Éléments d'Analyse Urbaine* (Brussels: Archives d'Architecture Moderne, 1980).

11 *Webster's New World College Dictionary*.

12 Auguste Choisy, *Histoire de l'Architecture* (Paris: Gauthier-Villars, 1899).

13 This was also the case for a contemporary of Choisy: Camillo Sitte, *City Planning According to Artistic Principles* (London: Phaidon Press, 1965 [orig. 1889]).

14 Gordon Cullen, *The Concise Townscape* (London: Van Nostrand Reinhold Company, 1961).

15 Kevin Lynch, *The Image of the City* (Cambridge, MA: MIT Press, 1960).

16 *Webster's New World College Dictionary*.

17 Robert Venturi, Denise Scott Brown and Steven Izenour, *Learning from Las Vegas: The Forgotten Symbolism of Architectural Form* (Cambridge, MA: MIT Press, 1977).

18 Beatriz Colomina, 'Learning from Levittown: A Conversation with Robert Venturi and Denise Scott Brown', in: Andrew Blauvelt (ed.), *Worlds Away, New Suburban Landscapes* (Minneapolis: Walker Art Center, 2008), 49–69.

19 Colomina, 'Learning from Levittown', 49–69.

20 Bruno Taut, *Die Neue Wohnung: Die Frau Als Schöpferin* (Leipzig: Klinkhardt & Biermann, 1924).

21 Tom Avermaete, 'Epistemologists of the Everyday', in: Tom Avermaete, *Another Modern: The Postwar Architecture and Urbanism of Candilis-Josic-Woods* (Rotterdam: Nai Publishers, 2005), 67–120.

22 Zeynep Çelik, 'Learning from the Bidonville: CIAM Looks at Algiers', *Harvard Design Magazine* 18 (Spring–Winter 2003), 70–74.

Bibliography

Argan, Giulio Carlo, 'On the Typology of Architecture', *Architectural Design* (December 1963), 564–565

Avermaete, Tom, 'Epistemologists of the Everyday', in: Tom Avermaete, *Another Modern: The Postwar Architecture and Urbanism of Candilis-Josic-Woods* (Rotterdam: Nai Publishers, 2005), 67–120.

Banham, Mary, et al. (eds.), *A Critic Writes. Selected Essays by Reynek Banham* (Los Angeles: University of California Press, 1996)

Cataldi, Giancarlo, Gian Luigi Maffei and Paola Vaccaro, 'Saverio Muratori and the Italian School of Planning Typology', *Urban Morphology* 6:1 (2002), 3–14

Çelik, Zeynep, 'Learning from the Bidonville: *CIAM* Looks at Algiers', *Harvard Design Magazine* 18 (Spring–Winter 2003), 70–74

Choisy, Auguste, *Histoire De L'architecture* (Paris: Gauthier-Villars, 1899)

Colomina, Beatriz, 'Learning from Levittown: A Conversation with Robert Venturi and Denise Scott Brown', in: Andrew Blauvelt (ed.), *Worlds Away, New Suburban Landscapes* (Minneapolis: Walker Art Center, 2008), 49–69

Colquhoun, Alan, 'Modern Architecture and the Symbolic Dimension of the Type and its Transformation', in: Alan Colquhoun, *Essays in Architectural Criticism: Modern Architecture and Historical Change* (Cambridge, MA; London: MIT Press, 1989), 43–50

Cullen, Gordon, *The Concise Townscape* (London: Van Nostrand Reinhold Company, 1961)

Durand, Jean-Nicolas-Louis, *Recueil et Parallèle des Édifices de Tout Genre, Anciens et Modernes* (Paris: Chez l'auteur, à l'école Polytechnique, 1801)

Durand, Jean-Nicolas-Louis, *Précis des Leçons d'Architecture Données à l'École Polytechnique* (Paris: Durand, 1802)

Foucault, Michel, Colin Gordon, *Power/Knowledge: Selected Interviews and Other Writings, 1972-1977* (New York: Pantheon Books, 1980)

Krier, Rob, 'Typological and Morphological Elements of the Concept of Space', in: Rob Krier, *Urban Space* (London: Academy Editions, 1988), 22–61

Lynch, Kevin, *The Image of the City* (Cambridge, MA: MIT Press, 1960)

Moneo, Rafael, 'On Typology', *Oppositions* 13 (Summer, 1978), 23–44

Muratori, Saverio, *Studi Per Una Operante Storia Urbana Di Venezia* (Roma: Istituto Poligrafico dello Stato, 1960)

Panerai, Philippe, Jean Castex and Jean-Charles Depaule, *Éléments d'Analyse Urbaine* (Brussels: Archives d'Architecture Moderne, 1980)

Rossi, Aldo, 'Problems of Classification', in: Aldo Rossi, *The Architecture of the City* (Cambridge, MA; London: MIT Press, 1992 [orig. 1966]), 48–54

Sitte, Camillo, *City Planning According to Artistic Principles* (London: Phaidon Press, 1965 [orig. 1889])

Taut, Bruno, *Die Neue Wohnung: Die Frau Als Schöpferin* (Leipzig: Klinkhardt & Biermann, 1924)

Venturi, Robert, Denise Scott Brown and Steven Izenour, *Learning from Las Vegas: The Forgotten Symbolism of Architectural Form* (Cambridge, MA: MIT Press, 1977)

Vidler, Anthony, 'The Third Typology', *Oppositions* 7 (1976), 1–4.

Webster's New World College Dictionary

Design Knowledges on the Move

Margitta Buchert

In the manifold spectrum of revealing tacit knowing in architecture, attention is directed here towards modalities for generating design and research knowledges and competences. How is it possible to shed some light on the specific nature of the forms of expertise practised in the interplay of experience, creative analyses and architectural design and research products? This expertise appears to be shaped in many ways. It might be seen as a network capability that connects different features linked to a property of an individual or of an organized group (a design and/or research team), a given body of knowledge, an acquired skill set, a complex interaction of instruments and human actors or a disciplinary habitus, just to name a few crucial shares.[1] Are there, in addition, some properties, alignments as well as specific experiential tools that can help to improve the process of high-quality design and research in general or, at any rate, some of its parts? This essay will discuss the resources of tacit knowing, focusing on *embodiment, empathy and the relevance of reflexive capacities* as a strategic research site to uncover and expound some characteristics that in this context, might provide a background and stimulate the further exploration of tacit knowing. Insight will be gained from philosophical, sociological and anthropological backgrounds as well as from more recent research in psychology and cognitive sciences, and finally from dance research, in order to propose clues for inquiries, as well as modalities for thought and action.

Zoom in on the perceptual

Tacit dimensions, as part and parcel of practice, have been described by the medically trained Hungarian chemist and philosopher Michael

Polanyi since the late 1950s as a specific way of knowing. In his perspective, this form of knowing 'indwells' in the confluence of mind and body, and is generated by focal as well as subsidiary awareness of context and haptic experience.² Perception, movement and bodily interactions with the environment, as well as features of cognition, are addressed. In Polanyi's view, the body is always there, providing a tacit fund whereby body and mind are configured modes of lived reality.³ By focusing on relations between knowers and known, and also between actors and tools as a kind of immersion, Polanyi wanted both to shed light on the complex phenomena of embodied knowledge and bring reality into focus as a creative discovery based on encounters.⁴ Furthermore, he promoted not only the protection of unrestricted individual thought but also the embeddedness of that individual within a community, and suggested exploring and refining the relationships of these realms and of shared values.⁵

These compact and abstract descriptions outline a complex configuration, which at the same time seems tacitly understandable. However, the highlighted meaning of the body-mind-environment realms opens up a broad range of additional questions. Here, the thoughts of the French philosopher Maurice Merleau-Ponty may provide a further point of consideration. Not only is the work of Merleau-Ponty referenced by Polanyi but it has also maintained a persistent impact on artistic, design and research practices, even though the focuses and interpretations have different perspectives and have somewhat changed over time.⁶ While the aim of Polanyi was to gain knowledge on dimensions of different kinds of knowing, Merleau-Ponty´s driving interest was more to uncover lived dimensions of experience.⁷

In his 1945 magnum opus *Phenomenology of Perception*, and as well in his posthumously published thoughts *The Visible and the Invisible*, Merleau-Ponty described the factual existence of a human being, which is perceived on a sensuous-physical level, as fundamental for raising awareness.⁸ The unfolding experience is based on the embodied presence in a field of relations as an instrument to be anchored in the world, to configure with it and to make it accessible over time through the dynamic emergence of understanding. Hereby, Merleau-Ponty opted for a plurality of being and recognized the sense of identity and meaningful qualities of an active and contextually embedded perception and its continual reset and revitalizing character.⁹ Intersubjectivity and sociality with the other are integrated into an embodied understanding including the pre-existing past and leading to a dynamic imagination of differently composed multiple experiences. With these perspectives, he avoided a strong form of biological essentialism, which critics nevertheless sometimes ascribe to him.¹⁰

Furthermore, Merleau-Ponty's objective was not only to reveal grounds for experiencing but also to highlight the capacity of reaching beyond existing structures in order to generate others.¹¹ Because Merleau-Ponty embraces the ability to surmount the immediate environment and be settled between real and possible worlds in a balanced way, his studies can be important in the twenty-first century in terms of fluid definitions of the individual, of balancing orientation and disorientation, and at the same time of differentiation.¹² In the end, he invited an understanding of vagueness as a positive phenomenon and linked it to artistic ways of producing alterity to extend, challenge or change perceptions of realities; a competence, which he named 'sur-réflexion'.¹³

Here, the perspective opens up to connect the intent of uncovering tacit knowledges with inventive settings and acting in novel ways to various arising questions. The notion of corporeality and perception in relation to the researcher and the researched context could be conceived as part and parcel of these investigations to generate crucial insights, create knowledges and guide inspiration, thus being aware that perception is not a matter of fully recognizing but a potentiality that has to be observed in many ways and explored in more differentiated manners.

Relate embodiment and cognition

Within this spectrum, the considerations of Merleau-Ponty and Polanyi anticipated some insights into phenomena that had recently unfolded in the context of various evidence-based and analytic discourses on cognition and knowledge generation. Thus, the concepts of embodied cognition, which include bodily sensorimotor capacities as a considerable part of its configuration as well as the entanglement of mind and bodily actions, have been actualized and enhanced in studies on cognitive sciences, psychology and philosophy, and have also found broad resonance in architecture.[14] Cognitive scientists conceived cognition as the exercise of skilful know-how in embodied and situated action.[15] Processes of perceiving could outline perception as the coordination of behaviour between bodies and the environment, and be linked to the generation of patterns of behaviour, which in architectural design and research processes, for example, might include extensions by augmented tools.[16]

Having a body with various sensorimotor capacities causes, so it is assumed, experience which also generates skills such as reasoning, judgement and mental constructs.[17] In the cognitive view, then, perception is conceived as intermodal from the start and the result of interaction between body and environment, particularly of vision, the sense of touch and proprioception as well as action-oriented capabilities.[18] Yet, to what extent sediments of traditions of perception and socialized imprints of cultures are included might be questioned here. It also seems to be important to focus on concepts of subjectivity and individual autobiographical characteristics, on unique experiential knowing, and also to draw further insights from the growing discourse on non-human actors, such as matter, interpreted as being equipped with some kind of vital energy.[19]

In short, drawing on all these considerations, cognition appears to be less computation and representation in the first line – as often assumed – and more an issue of adaptation and interaction. The awareness of diversity and the openness for revealing varieties and partiality could be linked to these ideas.[20] But, aimed towards architecture, what kinds of knowing emerge along the way? How does the architect become attuned or calibrated to foster knowledges and capabilities specific to the field of architectural design activities and the qualities of their outcomes? And which features can be supportive?

With empathy

Varying levels of *Einfühlung/empathy* may offer one of the possible approaches to come closer to hidden modes and mechanisms of modalities in creative analyses and design practices. Empathy, in a nutshell, is widely regarded as the ability to understand and share and/or to imagine the feelings of another. Referring to the spectrum of comprehensions of the term empathy in interdisciplinary discourses of the last decades and their potential for studies in architecture, three main dimensions can be opened up, even though it is a heterogenous concept.[21] These are positions on, first, 'sensitive thinking', in order to comprehend human attitudes and behaviour in specific contemporary (or historical) conditions, second, aesthetical or ethical foundations, and finally, triggers for action.

Current concepts of the neurosciences surprisingly confirm some of the descriptions offered by researchers in medicine, psychology, art history and architectural theory since the mid-nineteenth century on Einfühlung/empathy as the capacity of feeling 'into' creatures and things. Thus, for instance, interpersonal human experiences are in part conceived as the direct physical comprehension of observed conditions by the concept of so-called mirror neurons.[22] While this might be described as basic empathy, linked to an attentive, sensitive perception of places, spaces and situations, re-enactive empathy can be considered as intermingled with cognitive processes and as more complex.

The latter might additionally be understood as bound to cultural impacts, as a safeguarding of inter-subjective value communication and a source of knowledge.[23] With regard to the realm of architecture, it is particularly interesting that the aesthetic dimension of empathy is closely connected to dealing with occupying, bodily perceiving and creating space, with embodied and emotive experiences, as well as the ethical dimensions that could be linked to patterns of social perception.[24]

For sure, in these realms, some dimensions cannot be displayed and thus will remain the (known) unknown. But for some others, a further explanation might be elucidating. Considered in the light of various research findings, one can conceive a distinction between empathy as contrived and disciplined experience linked to a planned action with guiding points of view, positing an internally represented knowledge structure – a body of knowns, rules, principles or propositions, which serves to guide the execution of the capacity. This capability is often interpreted as being socialized and discussed as a mixing of orientation, values, emotional drivers, bodily skills and so on.[25] On the other hand, empathy could also be conceived as an open-minded observation: as a kind of reading and creating.[26] In this understanding, the observing researcher and designer patiently perceives, records, registers and collects the sensuous issues of architecture's (vibrant) physicality and the environment, for example, by movement. Moreover, empathy-like features are to be found both in imagining the architectural designers' or design team's intentions for the observed environment and in anticipating other humans' perceptions by conceptualizing and designing new ones. This might be described as a disposition, which relates resonance and projection. The first variant seems more predictable; the latter more linked to the unforeseen. To encourage the emergence of knowledge in these processes, memory and imagination may also be taken into account.

Memory and imagination

Both phenomena are discussed in the context of movement and cognition studies, as well as in research fields on creativity. Moreover, as elements of the complex configuration of human activities, they have both been considered relevant to the further development of artificial intelligence and robotics. Memory, as a linkage to a possible that once was a real, can be activated in constructive processes. With proportions of modification, reconstruction and adaptation, it might fuse the past experience with new information. Imagination works in this as a mediating, interpreting and anticipating feature.[27] Research on dance, for example, has shown that in this art, where the movement of the body is essential, specific instruments of sensuous perception and imagination are continually enacted and form memory as part of processes of unfolding knowledge over time.[28] This, in turn, is able to generate an implicit awareness of possibilities for movement and other actions in a given context. Repeated movement thereby blends into layered patterns of behaviour. These kinds of memory might not only generate foundations for successful action but also, in the state of an experimental surplus, create innovative shaping.[29] In these contexts, connecting positions and states in sequences and processes plays a crucial role.[30]

Analogously, architectural imagination can be thought of as emerging from an individual repertoire, gained by sensorimotor perceptions and actions, and by memories related to the movement they have experienced, exercised and used to perform, and thus might improve the design execution of a new interpretation. There are distinctive 'individual capabilities' involved, shaped by life experiences such as travelling or social activities, and acquired especially through intense perception and observation by on-site inspection of architecture and the built environment, as well as in design processes in relation to manual design actions with diverse media such as, for example, drawing, writing or model-building.[31] Therefore, to explain the process of knowing in these contexts, deep readings of conditions, modalities, actions and interactions should be included. Finally, to conceive tacit knowing as a form of knowledge, we might expand the viewpoint with an alignment to 'successful action'. Between a plurality of design knowledges, which could be used to grasp the specific competencies of architects, as well as being crucial for their responsibilities in the shaping of human living environments, deep readings and lived experience have a huge potential to reveal tacit dimensions. In these realms, the physicality in the design process and the physicality of the built become a part of the living body as well as of the architectural designer's and researcher's thought.[32]

For design alignments

Le Corbusier, to cite only one well-known example, postulated that there is a distinction in the impact of architecture, depending on whether the movement through the built has been taken into account while designing or not, which shows that there is an awareness of such dimensions of tacit knowing in architecture, even if elements and features have not yet been worked out in a differentiated way.[33]

Architectural spaces that form and enclose – in contrast to artworks – the everyday reality of people's lives provide multisensory stimulation, whereby movement and the surrounding conditions function together as a precondition of social life. The value is that of a specific 'experience', which is linked to the observation and generation of qualities such as the variety of situations of the guiding 'route areas' and centralized 'place areas', and the transitions between them, by the interplay of indoor and outdoor, light and shade, confinement and expanse, spatial depth, rough and smooth characters of the materials, and so on. This could be seen as different kinds of melodies, which encourage diverse movements and experiences. The way in which architectural elements and geometries are arranged – as straight, bent or curving forms, as sequential or rhythmic – the way in which the light or the attention is directed, and in which material qualities are shaped: all these have an effect on the sequence of movements and the individual, specific experience of architecture.[34] Current evidence-based research in the neurosciences, positioned at the intersection between medicine, humanities and arts, underlines this perspective by highlighting the relevance of environmental qualities that support sensation and perception, the modulation of emotion, communication and movement, as well as spaces for focused concentration and collaboration.[35]

The anticipation of the routes through architecture and of places, as well as the design of sequential structures with different stimulating qualities were described by Le Corbusier in the context of one of his prime values, with the 'promenade architecturale' as a tool of the architect, linked to both analysis and design.[36] This kind of 'aesthetic empathy' through kinaesthetic sensory perception is constituted via memory, current experience and expectation. The goal of these complex cognitive empathic processes is to increase the quality of the process and the product of design. The means are value settings, which act as triggers and are situated in physicality and cultural relations. Modalities such as empathy as skill, oscillating between inborn and acquired qualifications, generate the competence to reveal and handle built spatial qualities. As perceptions, sensations or imaginations, they might be hidden. By reflexivity – as a further modality – they are stored in the mind or might be further developed and concretized in sketches, models, photography or words as kinds of archives, which will be tacit or explicit sources of further thought and design action.

By reflexivity

The specificities of knowledge performance through reflexivity lead to a transdisciplinary research field, which since the 1990s has increasingly and extensively discussed reflexivity as a configuration of features for mature research. Reflexivity goes beyond what urbanist and researcher Donald Schön proposed as reflection 'in' action from the 1980s on, be it as phases or moments in design or research processes.[37] Reflection in action feeds back and improves the outcome. Reflexivity, in short, is discussed as an attitude, an approach and a tool for a more comprehensive reflection 'on' action, already mentioned by Schön.[38] This orientation encourages a more systematic approach and a heightened awareness of goals, conditions, driving forces, entanglements, outcomes, limitations and potentials.

These viewpoints can be extended to refer to discourse fields of the humanities, especially the social sciences, psychology and education.[39] It comes to the fore that certain degrees of reflexivity might enhance the understanding of present states, enhance capacities to act and foster innovative ways of creating knowledge, as it was presented in detail, with a continuing impact, by anthropologist and social scientist Pierre Bourdieu, as well as by the time diagnostically based concept of a 'reflexive modernity', postulated by Anthony Giddens, Scott Lash and Ulrich Beck.[40] These discourses advocate the role of criticality in connection with reflexivity but also the imaginative powerful trigger it could be. Transferred to an architectural design perspective, it directs the attention to what architecture is able to bring about in the realm of reception and to what architecture might be in the realm of conception. It thereby includes the intention to improve qualities in constituting the human living environment in different cultural contexts: in short, to confluence the observing body with a sensitivity towards local culture and the actual and historical situation.[41]

In this lens, a kind of codified disciplinary knowledge and habitus have to be completed by self-reflexivity, which is more discussed in the scientific field of cognitive sciences, philosophy and aesthetics as supporting attitudes and capabilities. In particular, the removal of the body and mind divide, which has, since centuries, been the leading conception of sciences and worldviews, is questioned in these perspectives. Against this background, reflexivity can be thought through and used on three levels. First, it can be conceived as a questioning of habitus, as a socialized knowledge base which might be explicit or implicit, and mixings of these two types of appearance. Second, it can be read as an instrument of self-awareness and improvement. And finally, reflexivity might be developed as 'sur-réflexion' to show and generate unimagined states.

On the move

These considerations on provisional variations of relating embodiment, empathy and reflexive capacities as compartments of design knowledges by opening up questions of modality might offer a background and stepping-stones for exploring dimensions of tacit knowing in architecture. Embodiment, empathy and reflexivity are some of the modalities present in practice that can foster the transformation of experience into a successful tool and trigger knowledge conversion, rendering tacit knowing explicit.[42] Combined, they make it possible to uncover both the uniqueness and particularities of different embodiments, as well as some overarching correlations. Moreover, implicit and explicit ways of knowing could be enhanced in design and research processes and products to show their powerful character as opening up insights into alternative and new practices, as interactive and open-ended, as dynamic and on the move.

Notes

1. Margitta Buchert (ed.), *Practices of Reflexive Design* (Berlin: Jovis, 2016); Margitta Buchert (ed.), *Processes of Reflexive Design* (Berlin: Jovis, 2018).
2. Michael Polanyi, *The Tacit Dimension* (New York: Doubleday, 1966), 55, 148.
3. See also Kyle Tataki, 'Enactive Realism', *Tradition and Discovery: The Polanyi Society Periodical* 38:1 (2011), 50.
4. Michael Polanyi, *Knowing and Being* (Chicago: The University of Chicago Press, 1969), 123–138.
5. Tilhamér Margitay, 'Introduction', in: Tilhamér Margitay (ed.), *Knowing and Being. Perspectives on the Philosophy of Michael Polanyi* (Newcastle upon Tyne: Cambridge Scholars, 2010), 4.
6. For current interpretations see, for example, Bryan E. Norwood, 'Disorienting Phenomenology', *Log* 42 (2018), 10–22; Alberto Perez-Gomez, *Attunement* (Cambridge, MA: MIT Press, 2016).
7. Tataki, 'Enactive Realism', 52–58.
8. Maurice Merleau-Ponty, *Phenomenology of Perception* (London: Routledge, 2012 [orig. 1945, German translation 1966]), 102; Maurice Merleau-Ponty, *Das Sichtbare und das Unsichtbare* [The Visible and the Invisible], 2nd ed. (München: Fink, 1994), 153–159, 314.
9. Merleau-Ponty, *Das Sichtbare und das Unsichtbare*, 273–274; Merleau-Ponty *Phenomenology of Perception*, 102, 186.
10. See, for example, Jorge Otero-Pailos, *Architecture's Historical Turn. Phenomenology and the Rise of the Postmodern* (Minneapolis: University of Minnesota, 2010), 139; Norwood, 'Disorienting Phenomenology', 13–18.

11 Maurice Merleau-Ponty, *The Structure of Behavior* (London: Beacon Press, 1963), 47, 175; Merleau-Ponty, *Das Sichtbare und das Unsichtbare*, 137–138, 158; and further Margitta Buchert, 'Spielräume im Unbestimmten', in: Margitta Buchert and Carl Zillich (eds.), *Inklusiv. Architektur und Kunst* (Berlin: Jovis, 2006), 53–59.

12 Merleau-Ponty, *Das Sichtbare und das Unsichtbare*, 51, 78–83.

13 See, for example, ibid., 76; Laura Huber, *Der Philosoph und der Künstler. Merleau-Ponty als Denker der 'Réflexion'* (Würzburg: Königshausen und Neumann, 2013), 142–152.

14 See, for example, Harry Francis Mallgrave, *The Architect's Brain. Neuroscience, Creativity and Architecture* (Malden, MA: Wiley-Blackwell, 2010); Juhani Pallasmaa and Sarah Robinson (eds.), *Mind in Architecture. Neuroscience, Embodiment and the Future of Design* (Cambridge, MA: MIT Press, 2015).

15 Gregor Etzelmüller, Thomas Fuchs and Christian Tewes, 'Introduction', in: Gregor Etzelmüller, Thomas Fuchs and Christian Tewes, (eds.), *Verkörperung als Paradigma einer neuen Anthropologie* (Berlin: de Gruyter, 2007), 8–9.

16 Humberto R. Maturana and Francisco J. Varela, *The Tree of Knowledge. Biological Roots of Human Understanding* (Boston, MA: Shambhala, 1992), 239–245; and further Jonathan Hale, *Merleau-Ponty for Architects* (London: Routledge, 2017), 89–90.

17 Francisco J. Varela, Eleanor Rosch and Evan Thompson, *The Embodied Mind* (Cambridge, MA: MIT Press, 2016), 172–173.

18 Shaun Gallagher, *How the Body Shapes the Mind* (Oxford: Clarendon, 2005), 160, 170.

19 On the relevance of the individual, see, for example, Paul Dumouchel, 'Embodiment. The Ecology of Mind', *Philosophies* 4 (2019), 12; on vibrant environmental realms, see Donna Haraway, *The Reinvention of Nature* (New York: Routledge, 1991), 184–192; Maxime Sheets-Johnstone, 'Foundational Dynamics of Animate Nature', in: Undine Eberlein (ed.), *Zwischenleiblichkeit und bewegtes Verstehen. Incorporeality, Movement and Tacit Knowledge* (Bielefeld: Transcript, 2016), 57–58; Lambros Malafouris, *How Things Shape the Mind. A Theory of Material Engagement* (Cambridge, MA: MIT Press, 2013), 153–226.

20 See, for example, Sara Ahmed, *On Being Included* (Durham: Duke University Press, 2012), 173–187.

21 Eva Köppen, *Empathy by Design* (Konstanz: UVK, 2016), 23–103.

22 Chris Abel, 'The Extended Self. Tacit Knowing and Place Identity', in: Ritu Bhatt (ed.), *Rethinking Aesthetics. The Role of Body in Design* (New York: Routledge, 2013), 119–128; Harry Francis Mallgrave, *Architecture and Embodiment. The Implications of the New Sciences and Humanities for Design* (London: Routledge, 2013), 120–174.

23 Karsten R. Stueber, *Rediscovering Empathy, Agency, Folk Psychology, and the Human Sciences* (Cambridge, MA: MIT Press, 2006), 7–148.

24 Mallgrave, *Architecture and Embodiment*; Philip Tidwell (ed.), *Architecture and Empathy* (Espoo: Tapio Wirkkala Rut Bryk Foundation, 2015).

25 Derek Maltravers, *Empathy* (Cambridge: Polity, 2017), 28.

26 Shaun Gallagher, 'Empathy and Theories of Direct Action', in: Heidi Maiblom (ed.), *The Routledge Handbook of Philosophy of Empathy* (London: Routledge, 2017), 158–168.

27 Tsofit Ofengenden, *Memory and Imagination. Epistemological Perspectives from British Empiricists to Neuroscience* (Tübingen: UB, 2016), 7–10, 247–248.

28 Gallagher, *How the Body Shapes the Mind*, 160–165.

29 Michael Arbib, 'Toward a Neuroscience of the Design Process', in: Juhani Pallasmaa and Sarah Robinson (eds.), *Mind in Architecture. Neuroscience, Embodiment and the Future of Design* (Cambridge, MA: MIT Press, 2015), 92–97; Stephan Brinkmann, *Bewegung erinnern. Gedächtnisformen im Tanz* (Bielefeld: Transcript, 2013), 40–66; and further Volker Caysa, 'Körperliche Erkenntnis als empraktische Körpererinnerung', in: Franz Bockrath,

Bernhard Boschert and Elk Franke (eds.), *Körperliche Erkenntnis. Formen reflexiver Erfahrung* (Bielefeld: Transcript, 2008), 77–79.

30 Deidre Sklar, 'Five Premises for a Culturally Sensitive Approach to Dance', in: Ann Cooper Albright and Ann Dils, *Moving History. Dancing Cultures* (Middletown CT: Wesleyan University Press, 2001), 31.

31 See for example Juhani Pallasmaa, *The Thinking Hand* (Chichester: Wiley and Sons, 2009), 88–105; Karen Moon, *Modelling Messages. The Architect and the Model* (New York: Monacelli Press, 2005), 161–186.

32 On traditions of such perspectives, see, for example, Gilles Deleuze, *Spinoza* (Berlin: Merve, 1988), 27–29, 45.

33 Le Corbusier, *An die Studenten* (Reinbek, Hamburg: Rowohlt, 1962), 29–30.

34 Margitta Buchert, 'Mobile and Stabile', in: Annett Zinsmeister, *Figure of Motion* (Berlin: Jovis, 2011), 48–73.

35 Eve Edelstein, 'Neuroscience and Architecture', in: Mitra Kanaani and Dak Kopec (eds.), *The Routledge Companion for Architecture Design and Practice* (New York: Routledge, 2016), 284.

36 Le Corbusier, *An die Studenten*.

37 Donald A. Schön, *The Reflective Practitioner. How Professionals Think in Action*, 3rd ed. (London: Ashgate, 2003), 39–69.

38 Ibid. and 276–281.

39 See, for example, Tim May and Beth Perry, *Reflexivity* (London: Sage, 2017).

40 Pierre Bourdieu, *Science de la Science et Réflexivité* (Paris: Raisons d'Agir Éditions, 2001), 174–184; Ulrich Beck, Anthony Giddens and Scott Lash, *Reflexive Modernisierung. Eine Kontroverse* (Frankfurt am Main: Suhrkamp, 1996).

41 Margitta Buchert, 'Reflexive Design. Topologies of a Research Field', in: Margitta Buchert (ed.), *Reflexive Design. Design and Research in Architecture* (Berlin: Jovis, 2014), 24–49.

42 See also Brian Massumi, *The Principle of Unrest. Activist Philosophy in the Expanded Field* (London: Open Humanities Press, 2017), 42, 51.

Bibliography

Abel, Chris, 'The Extended Self. Tacit Knowing and Place Identity', in: Ritu Bhatt (ed.), *Rethinking Aesthetics. The Role of Body in Design* (New York: Routledge, 2013), 101–139

Ahmed, Sara, *On Being Included* (Durham: Duke University Press, 2012)

Arbib, Michael, 'Toward a Neuroscience of the Design Process', in: Juhani Pallasmaa and Sarah Robinson, *Mind in Architecture. Neuroscience, Embodiment and the Future of Design* (Cambridge, MA: MIT Press, 2015), 75–98

Beck, Ulrich, Anthony Giddens and Scott Lash, *Reflexive Modernisierung. Eine Kontroverse* (Frankfurt am Main: Suhrkamp, 1996)

Bourdieu, Pierre, *Science de la Science et Réflexivité* (Paris: Raisons d'Agir Éditions, 2001)

Brinkmann, Stephan, *Bewegung erinnern. Gedächtnisformen im Tanz* (Bielefeld: Transcript, 2013), 40–66

Buchert, Margitta, 'Spielräume im Unbestimmten', in: Margitta Buchert and Carl Zillich (eds.), *Inklusiv. Architektur und Kunst* (Berlin: Jovis, 2006), 53–59

Buchert, Margitta 'Mobile and Stabile', in: Annett Zinsmeister, *Figure of Motion* (Berlin: Jovis, 2011), 48–73

Design Knowledges on the Move 95

Buchert, Margitta, 'Reflexive Design. Topologies of a Research Field', in: Margitta Buchert (ed.), *Reflexive Design. Design and Research in Architecture* (Berlin: Jovis, 2014), 24–49

Buchert, Margitta (ed.), *Practices of Reflexive Design* (Berlin: Jovis, 2016)

Buchert, Margitta (ed.), *Processes of Reflexive Design* (Berlin: Jovis, 2018)

Caysa, Volker, 'Körperliche Erkenntnis als empraktische Körpererinnerung', in: Franz Bockrath, Bernhard Boschert and Elk Franke (eds.), *Körperliche Erkenntnis. Formen reflexiver Erfahrung* (Bielefeld: Transcript, 2008), 73–85

Deleuze, Gilles, *Spinoza* (Berlin: Merve, 1988)

Dumouchel, Paul, 'Embodiment. The Ecology of Mind', *Philosophies* 4:2 (2019), 12–19

Edelstein, Eve, 'Neuroscience and Architecture', in: Mitra Kanaani and Dak Kopec (eds.), *The Routledge Companion for Architecture Design and Practice* (New York: Routledge, 2016), 269–287

Etzelmüller, Gregor, Thomas Fuchs and Christian Tewes, 'Introduction', in: Gregor Etzelmüller, Thomas Fuchs and Christian Tewes, (eds.), *Verkörperung als Paradigma einer neuen Anthropologie* (Berlin: de Gruyter, 2007), 1–30

Gallagher, Shaun, *How the Body Shapes the Mind* (Oxford: Clarendon, 2005)

Gallagher, Shaun, 'Empathy and Theories of Direct Action', in: Heidi Maiblom (ed.), *The Routledge Handbook of Philosophy of Empathy* (London: Routledge, 2017), 158–168

Haraway, Donna, *The Reinvention of Nature* (New York: Routledge, 1991)

Hale, Jonathan, *Merleau-Ponty for Architects* (London: Routledge, 2017)

Huber, Laura, *Der Philosoph und der Künstler. Merleau-Ponty als Denker der 'réflexion'* (Würzburg: Königshausen und Neumann, 2013)

Köppen, Eva, *Empathy by Design* (Konstanz: UVK, 2016)

Le Corbusier, *An die Studenten* (Reinbek b. Hamburg: Rowohlt, 1962)

Malafouris, Lambros, *How Things Shape the Mind. A Theory of Material Engagement* (Cambridge, MA: MIT Press, 2013)

Mallgrave, Harry Francis, *The Architect's Brain. Neuroscience, Creativity and Architecture* (Malden, MA: Wiley-Blackwell, 2010)

Mallgrave, Harry Francis, *Architecture and Embodiment. The Implications of the New Sciences and Humanities for Design* (London: Routledge, 2013)

Maltravers, Derek, *Empathy* (Cambridge: Polity, 2017)

Margitay, Tilhamér, 'Introduction', in: Tilhamér Margitay (ed.), *Knowing and Being. Perspectives on the Philosophy of Michael Polanyi* (Newcastle upon Tyne: Cambridge Scholars, 2010), 1–10

Massumi, Brian, *The Principle of Unrest. Activist Philosophy in the Expanded Field* (London: Open Humanities Press, 2017)

Maturana, Humberto R. and Francisco J. Varela, *The Tree of Knowledge. Biological Roots of Human Understanding* (Boston, MA: Shambhala, 1992)

May, Tim and Beth Perry, *Reflexivity* (London: Sage, 2017)

Merleau-Ponty, Maurice, *The Structure of Behavior* (London: Beacon Press, 1963)

Merleau-Ponty, Maurice, *Phenomenology of Perception* (London: Routledge, 2012 [orig. 1945, German translation 1966])

Merleau-Ponty, Maurice, *Das Sichtbare und das Unsichtbare* [The Visible and the Invisible], 2nd ed. (München: Fink, 1994)

Moon, Karen, *Modelling Messages. The Architect and the Model* (New York: Monacelli Press, 2005)

Norwood, Bryan E., 'Disorienting Phenomenology', *Log* 42 (2018), 10–22

Ofengenden, Tsofit, *Memory and Imagination. Epistemological Perspectives from British Empiricists to Neuroscience* (Tübingen: UB, 2016)

Otero-Pailos, Jorge, *Architecture's Historical Turn. Phenomenology and the Rise of the Postmodern* (Minneapolis: University of Minnesota, 2010)

Pallasmaa, Juhani, *The Thinking Hand* (Chichester: Wiley and Sons, 2009)

Pallasmaa, Juhani and Sarah Robinson (eds.), *Mind in Architecture. Neuroscience, Embodiment and the Future of Design* (Cambridge, MA: MIT Press, 2015)

Perez-Gomez, Alberto, *Attunement* (Cambridge, MA: MIT Press, 2016)

Polanyi, Michael, *The Tacit Dimension* (New York: Doubleday, 1966)

Polanyi, Michael, *Knowing and Being* (Chicago: The University of Chicago Press, 1969)

Schön, Donald A., *The Reflective Practitioner. How Professionals Think in Action*, 3rd ed. (London: Ashgate, 2003)

Sheets-Johnstone, Maxime, 'Foundational Dynamics of Animate Nature', in: Undine Eberlein (ed.), *Zwischenleiblichkeit und bewegtes Verstehen. Incorporeality, Movement and Tacit Knowledge* (Bielefeld: Transcript, 2016), 51–67

Sklar, Deidre, 'Five Premises for a Culturally Sensitive Approach to Dance', in: Ann Cooper Albright and Ann Dils, *Moving History. Dancing Cultures* (Middletown CT: Wesleyan University Press, 2001), 30–32

Stueber, Karsten R., *Rediscovering Empathy, Agency, Folk Psychology, and the Human Sciences* (Cambridge, MA: MIT Press, 2006)

Tataki, Kyle, 'Enactive Realism', *Tradition and Discovery* 38:1 (2011), 43–59

Tidwell, Philip (ed.), *Architecture and Empathy* (Espoo: Tapio Wirkkala Rut Bryk Foundation, 2015)

Varela, Francisco J., Eleanor Rosch and Evan Thompson, *The Embodied Mind* (Cambridge, MA: MIT Press, 2016)

A Silent Master: Artistry and Craft in the Work of Peter Celsing

Christoph Grafe

'Nonetheless Celsing is in no way a 'popular' architect, rather he is aristocratic and exclusive'.[1] It was with these few words that Henrik Andersson, a former director of the Swedish Architectural Museum, characterized Peter Celsing in the first book dedicated to an architect who has become something of a key figure in the alternative modern canon of the past three decades.[2] The author continues: 'when he was made professor at the Stockholm Polytechnic about twenty years ago, his name was above all connected to his achievement as a church architect. He had almost no contact with the large working tasks that occupied many architects at this time: housing, schools, hospitals or town planning'. Among his fellow architects, Celsing was encountered with 'great interest and respect' but clearly viewed as a highly individual architect in a profession that saw itself as part of the concrete collective programme of building the everyday environment of the welfare state. That this architect would become the designer of a building that was to put the crown on the building production of modern Stockholm and in a way represented the climax of the egalitarian programme of Swedish Social Democracy must have seemed an ironic twist of fate to many of those who had devoted their professional lives to building within the collective mainstream of Swedish architecture in the mid-sixties.[3] Perhaps ironically, the Kulturhus turned out to be a last outpouring of an architectural culture dominated by a series of generations of – exclusively male – individuals: for a programme that may well be seen to embody an attack on exactly the kind of cultural network and professional value system of which Celsing was a late representative. The result of this constellation is an extraordinary architectural evocation of modernity and

Fig. 1. Stockholms Kulturhuset and Sergels Torg (photo Christoph Grafe, 2012).

Fig. 2. The Kulturhus was conceived as a living room for the city and remains to be used in this way (photo Christoph Grafe, 2012).

metropolitanism, rooted in memory and successfully – poetically – anticipating a new urban reality and an egalitarian society (Figs. 1-2).

Born in 1920 into a family with a formidable history,[4] Peter Celsing grew up in Östermalm, a neighbourhood that had been adopted by Stockholm's upper and upper-middle classes at the end of the nineteenth century. The family spent the summers in a second home at Drottningholm, a village – now suburb – around the summer residence of the Swedish royal family and a preferred summer retreat for architects. As Bergengren noted, Celsing grew up among objects that embodied one of the 'golden ages' of Swedish history.[5] He was acquainted with the custodian of the royal household's extensive store and the Drottningholm court theatre, which in the 1930s was being discovered as a unique remnant of eighteenth-century court culture. At the age of 16, Celsing spent some time in the architectural office of the Royal Palace, then directed by Ivar Tengbom, and enrolled as a student at Kungliga Tekniska Högskolan (KTH, the Royal Polytechnic School in Stockholm) in 1938. As a student, Celsing would just have been able to have a personal encounter with Gunnar Asplund before the latter fell terminally ill, but this is not recorded. Other influential teachers at KTH were Eskil Sundahl, one of the authors of *Acceptera*, the seminal text marking the introduction of continental modern architecture in Sweden, Erik Ahlsén, then one of the leading figures in KF, the cooperative movement's architects office, and his brother Tore.[6] The teacher to occupy a central role in the education of Celsing was Sven-Ivar Lind, who had collaborated with Asplund and took responsibility for completing projects such as the Skogskyrkogård (Woodland Cemetery) when the architect died in 1940.

Celsing graduated from KTH in 1943. In the previous year, he had travelled to Rome to study at the Swedish Institute – a fairly implausible journey given the general situation in Europe – and on his return, joined the prestigious School of Architecture at the Stockholm Academy of Art while working in the offices of Ivar Tengbom and Sven Ivar Lind, among others. In 1946, Celsing went abroad again, working for an architectural office in Beirut, and visited various Middle Eastern countries, including Istanbul, where one of his ancestors had been a Swedish diplomat. After his return to Stockholm, he worked in the planning department of the Stockholm Traffic Board on a series of stations for the rapidly expanding underground railway system. It was a series of competitions for new churches, three of which he managed to win, that allowed Celsing to set up his own firm in Stockholm.

Eventually, only one of these churches was realized, but it was this project that immediately afforded its designer with a position as a young notable architect. It was also in designing for the Swedish state church that Celsing collaborated with Sigurd Lewerentz, who had designed the Skogskyrkogård (Woodland Cemetery) with Gunnar Asplund; in 1951–52 the young architect and his much older colleague were entrusted with restoring the cathedral of Uppsala, the see of the primate of the Swedish Lutheran church and the burial place of kings and bishops.[7]

Churches and public works

During much of the 1950s and early 1960s, Celsing's attention was focused on the design of churches. These projects were part of the general building campaigns for the satellite towns and suburbs of the larger cities, and offered architects an opportunity of avoiding the standardized practice that characterized other fields of the building production. Church building allowed the architect to explore a large range of crafts and techniques that had become abandoned in larger-scale projects for housing or schools. For Celsing, the series of churches, which he designed in these years and most of which were completed between 1958 and 1960, marked a phase of intensive artistic experimentation within a defined architectural programme.

As a building task that from the outset related to tradition, both ideologically and in terms of liturgy, the construction of churches seemed to also invite thoughts on how existing or traditional typologies and building techniques could be reinvented in the context of new settlements. The projects for churches in the Gothenburg suburb of Härlanda, Stockholm's first large satellite town Vällingby, and Almtuna near Uppsala constitute a catalogue of architectural and structural solutions concerning, among others, the expressive qualities of the brick wall, the tectonic articulation of apertures and the space-defining effects of light. These projects also allowed Celsing to collaborate closely with artists such as the sculptor Sivert Lindblom, who was later to work with him on the competition design for the Kulturhus. The projects for and inside the

Stockholm Traffic Board were accompanied by other smaller projects for personal friends. However artistically inclined, Celsing's practice was from the very beginning, highly socially embedded. While his work for the Traffic Board was part of the transformation of the city within the politics of the welfare state, the smaller projects continued an established tradition of crafted buildings for the Swedish state church and private clients. Celsing, in other words, seems to have been extraordinarily capable of mastering very different registers: working within a network of close-knit individuals in the smaller projects, while also successfully operating in the larger technocratic culture of the city's building and traffic departments.

The projects for the churches as well as those for a small number of renovations of older buildings in the centre of Stockholm realized in the same period gave Celsing a large degree of control. As well as designing the layout of the spaces and their material appearance, he was in charge of drawing furniture and fittings, all of which could be purpose-made for projects of this kind. This would have involved a deep knowledge not only of contemporary building technology but also of the traditional crafts of carpentry or working with, sometimes precious, metals. His approach to architecture, while modern in its formal language, was, therefore, the result of circumstances that were becoming exceptional in the Swedish building production of the late 1950s and early 1960s. Concentrating on building tasks that could be seen to be somewhat outside the mainstream of the large building production of this period, Celsing appears as a representative of a specific tradition in which the architect's role was that of a versatile and cultured designer of artistically refined buildings with a high cultural status and an attachment to established institutions such as the state church. In this sense, his career was similar to those of the generation of architects whose careers had started in the 1910s and 20s, including Gunnar Asplund and Sigurd Lewerentz.

The poetry of silent things

Peter Celsing was not a reader and even less a writer. For this architect, the most important books, according to his collaborator Jan Henriksson, were visual; the journals of the late eighteenth-century artist and writer

Carl August Ehrensvärd, with their sketches from Italian journeys, retained a particular interest for the architect.[8] The texts setting out a theoretical stance are two lectures delivered in the context of accepting a professorship at KTH in 1960. In his inaugural lecture titled 'Om Rummet' (About Space), he describes his artistic programme as a search for the elements that address the individual and the collective, both emotionally and intellectually. Celsing's exposé of his position opens with a description of Piero della Francesca's fresco depicting the Flagellation of Christ in the Ducal Palace at Urbino. The scene shows the main figures arranged in the middle ground surrounded by columns of a palace. The dimensions of the palace are unknown to the beholder, but the columns suggest that it might extend far beyond the visible section. Celsing uses this proposal of an indefinite, invisible extension as an illustration for the oppositional nature of what he calls 'the physical and the metaphysical space'. The former is measurable and 'quantitative', whereas the latter remains not measurable and 'qualitative'.[9] This quality, Celsing suggests rather than formulates, charges the architectural spaces that can be measured with an experiential quality beyond their own boundaries: 'we find ourselves in a force field (*kraftfält*), a metaphysical space'.[10]

Celsing combines the scientific metaphor of the electric field and its effect on the bodies inside it with a reference to the mobile sculptures of Alexander Calder, whose work had been shown in the influential exhibition *Rörelse i konsten* in 1961 at Moderna Museet. The architect compares these artworks with their disparate elements moving around one or more notional, but usually empty, centres, with the setting of the main ceremonial and monumental buildings of Central Stockholm around the open waters of inlets of the Baltic. His evocative description of the ensemble of the Palace, Riksdag, Opera House, National Museum, Dramaten and the buildings on Skeppsholmen (including Moderna Museet) is that of an urban panorama of separate incidents and directions, openings and enclosures, with the water surface as an open middle ground across which the relationships between the buildings and their institutions are tangible. The buildings are objects with geometric qualities but, Celsing explains, 'at the same time they are also signs, symbols, embodying the institutions'.[11] The description of this urban landscape, which marks the epicentres of power and prestige, of royal privilege and cultural tradition, evokes the image of a stage set, the buildings operating both as set pieces and protagonists in a *tableau vivant* representing Sweden. 'The classical forms under the northern European sky expose a will to become part of a common world culture'.[12]

The reference to the representative character of these buildings forms the prologue to a discussion of modern architecture and its emphasis on function. There is an explicit criticism of the pre-war functional tradition: 'our obsession with the requirements of use, which almost has the status of a cult, and their functional and formal aesthetic aspects, could be said to reflect a need to compensate for what the environment lacks in the architectural definition of spaces'.[13] This approach implies a reduction of architectural spaces to their measurable function and a limited understanding of their performance as environments within the wider culture. Celsing's project can be described as an act of reintroducing memory and association, which 'contribute to the metaphysical content of space'.[14]

The fact that Celsing questions what he views as a narrowing of the definition of use in Functionalism does not, however, imply a departure from the modern tradition as such. On the contrary, whenever the architect makes an attempt to identify alternative strategies to the one-dimensionality of functionalist architecture, the examples are from the modern canon. In the inaugural speech, it is the work of Le Corbusier, the Villa Savoye and the church at Ronchamp that are presented as buildings that are free of the self-limitations of functionalist modern architecture. The reassessment of the representational character of architecture is developed as an evolution of the modern repertoire. And even where a building task involves restoring an existing monumental building like a church, Celsing points out, this can only be successful if the designer refrains from a historicist approach and accepts that a meaningful architectural proposal inevitably involves taking a position towards the technology and requirements of the present day: 'it is naïve to believe that an environment can be fixed forever'.[15]

In another lecture titled *'Om betongen'* (On concrete, a given subject) delivered at KTH around the same time, Celsing reiterated the history of the building material and its role in the development of formal architectural languages in the twentieth century. Starting with a series of observations on the use of concrete in the late nineteenth-century redesign of Uppsala cathedral by Hugo Zettervall and describing its indebtedness to Viollet-le-Duc, Celsing identifies concrete as a material that allows the architect to realize buildings as Ur-gestures: a bridge as 'a leap over the depths', a hangar as 'gesture of protective covering', a house with an open plan facilitated by a concrete structure as 'liberation from conventions'.[16] This view of concrete as a material that offers the opportunity for buildings to become primary creative gestures, like those 'of the child's hand, his digging, shaping, patting hand', seems to operate within the established modern paradigm of thinking of architecture as unique and, by definition, implying a rupture with the past or, as Celsing put it, an 'expression of our boldest dreams'.[17] All these references betray an interest in architectural design as being rooted in a longer history. Even the reading of the church at Ronchamp in Celsing's account becomes 'the kind of shell the Crusaders took back home with them from the Holy Land' – a successful act of creating a historical mythology rather than an alien object without a past.[18] Concrete, in other words, is a means to be embraced, in order to establish links to tradition, without historicizing; Celsing's own design for the Kulturhus (1966-74) and the Filmhus (Swedish Film Institute, 1964-70) provide poignant examples of this approach.

Celsing's reference to Le Corbusier is characteristic of architectural discourses in the period, following in the footsteps of Sigfried Giedion's version of the history of modern architecture. Invoking Le Corbusier might be seen as nothing more than an obligatory and commonplace reference. However, the selection of the projects – the Villa Savoye, the church at Ronchamp, the monastery of La Tourette and, repeatedly, Chandigarh – is also revealing. The Corbusier celebrated here is the master of what Siegfried Giedion had proposed as an 'eternal present', an architecture that is rooted in an indiscriminate history, a timeless continuum of 'constancy and change'.[19] Although there is no evidence that Celsing knew Giedion's book, the concept of a de-historicized history, a tradition that is all the more powerful for not being reflected upon, seems to resonate very strongly in the work of the Swedish architect. Celsing produced, during his entire career, references that extend to classical and baroque buildings, the domed ceilings of Sir John Soane and Ottoman structures. The interest is, however, never art historical. The history of architecture is a *musée imaginaire* of references, which can and will be used to effect but never as imitation or quotation.

Architecture as artistic practice

The accounts of collaborators published as contributions to the 1980 book provide evidence for the pivotal role of intuition in Celsing's design approach and endorse the idea of the architect as artist. Jan Henriksson mentions the 'enormous world of imagination' materializing in an extraordinarily larger number of sketches of events, images or building solutions.[20] From around 1965, Celsing extended his range of techniques, which had previously been limited to drawing in pen and pencil, and started to use watercolours for sketches depicting not so much architectural forms or spaces but rather life scenes.[21] Henriksson remembers: 'when Peter arrived in the office in the mornings, and particularly after a holiday, he brought a folder with paintings, sketches and drawings'. Apparently he never stopped: 'his incredible talent followed him continuously'.[22] As Söve Olsson notes, some of these sketches were reminiscent of those made by scenographers, film or theatre directors.[23] They depicted scenes of the use of buildings and of social practices which situated the buildings within an imagined popular culture (Figs. 3–5). Celsing refers to scenes recognizable from popular urban institutions, such as luna parks, squares, theatres or beer gardens. In their pictorial arrangement,

Fig. 3. Peter Celsing, sketch for 'Köket' (the kitchen), one of the restaurants (courtesy of Celsingarkivet, Stockholm).

Fig. 4. Peter Celsing, sketch for 'Kilen', a variety theatre housed in Kulturhuset (courtesy of Celsingarkivet, Stockholm).

Fig. 5. Peter Celsing, sketch of a street scene. The proposed municipal theatre is on the left (courtesy of Celsingarkivet, Stockholm).

these illustrations resemble mass-produced prints of nineteenth-century urban interiors, while the colourful and abstract renditions of everyday situations recall pre-World War II posters promoting seaside resorts, fairs, or popular spas. Other sketches, for example those examining façade proportions or details of light fittings, are, by contrast, more conventional and show the architect as a craftsman in control of his material. Celsing's sketches, made while having lunch or dinner, in the evenings or weekends, were complemented by a considerable production of models: first in plaster, later in wood.

The sculptor Sivert Lindblom remembers that the models for the church tower at Vällingby, which he made for Celsing, constituted a veritable 'feuilleton' of at least forty study models, each examining a variation on an already established theme. Lindblom describes his collaboration with the architect as being exploited in a positive way: 'to learn from his ability to look'. Celsing is said to have had the capacity of finding solutions everywhere, not only in the material of architecture but also 'in the encounter of the entire reality with the imagination of man': the approach being intuitive rather than analytical.[24]

All three collaborators praise Celsing's abilities of judgement and his 'eye' for three-dimensional effects. For the larger projects, and especially for the Kulturhus, however, the architect was not prepared to rely on this alone and commissioned a series of full-scale models of particular solutions. Henriksson mentions that such models were made, for example, for the façade of the Kulturhus and the Riksbank, the ceilings of the exhibition floors and the stainless steel panels of the theatre volume.[25]

The architectural office was housed in a building in the old town and extended into the large former hall of a bank when, in 1968, the tight schedule for developing the Kulturhus/parliament project caused it to grow from two or three to 40 people, while retaining its organization of an atelier. None of the 'devoted collaborators' who worked literally continuously – 'days, evenings, holidays, almost the whole time', to quote Henriksson – and whose task it was to interpret Celsing's sketches had a clearly defined task or precise job description.[26] This organizational model of the architect's office contrasted starkly with the highly developed hierarchies and specializations that started to dominate professional practice in the late 1960s in Europe and North America. Celsing's practice, by contrast, retained its loose organization around its single

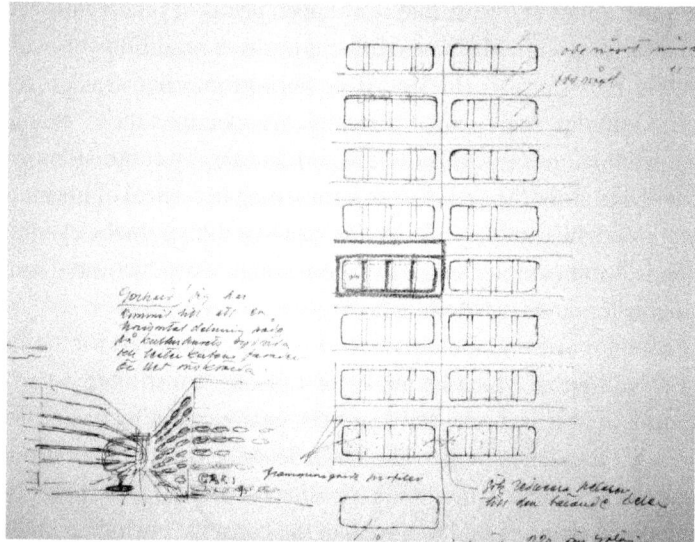

Fig. 6. Peter Celsing, sketch for a façade detail of the proposed theatre with instructions to collaborators in the practice. Celsing here proposes a horizontal organization for the façades on the south side and asks for adjustments to dimensioning the piers between the openings. (courtesy of Celsingarkivet, Stockholm).

Fig. 7. Stockholms Kulturhuset, façade municipal theatre (photo Christoph Grafe, 2012).

A Silent Master

'*inspirator* and master', even when the size of the commissions might have suggested something different in the late 1960s and early 70s (Figs. 6, 7).[27] The thesis formulated by Claes Caldenby, that Peter Celsing was a late – and possibly the last – representative of the Swedish tradition of master architects, is, therefore, supported by a manifest resistance to adopt the managerial models that were introduced in many other offices in this period. His authority resided both in the admiration of his collaborators, who tirelessly worked from the sketches and respected the principal for his abilities and his enormous work capacity, which inspired them to 'work well beyond our personal limitations'.[28] Celsing's *habitus* of a silent master was reciprocated in the *modus operandi* of his office, allowing his work to provide a poetry of the modern metropolis and to construct it.

Notes

1. Henrik O. Andersson, 'Peter Celsing – från tunnelbana till kulturhus', in: Beate Sydhoff et al. (eds.) *1930/80 – Arkitektur, Form, Konst*, exhibition catalogue (Stockholm: Kulturhuset, 1980), 76.

2. See also Claes Caldenby, 'The Time of the Large Programmes 1960–75', in: Claes Caldenby, Jöran Lindvall and Wilfried Wang (eds.) *Sweden — Twentieth-Century Architecture*. (Munich/New York: Prestel, 1998), 155.

3. From 1965, half the volume of the Swedish building production had been part of the so-called 'Million Programme' that entailed the standardized and industrialized production of one million homes across the whole of the country. This large-scale campaign was one of the decisive factors for the structural change in the Swedish building industries in the period and the concentration of its activities in a relatively small number of very large corporations. Claes Caldenby 'The Time of the Large Programmes', 145–47.

4. In the Swedish Biographical Encyclopaedia, the Celsing family has an extensive entry. In the eighteenth century, two ancestors operated as royal Swedish envoys at the High Gate in Constantinople, one of Sweden's allies ('Turkiets äldste vän', 'Turkey's oldest friend') in its policies to retain the status of the major power in Northern Europe against Russia and Denmark. Later, the family's focus shifted towards business and early industrial production. Bertil Boëthius, (ed.), *Svenskt Biografiskt Lexikon*, vol. 18 (Stockholm: Albert Bonnier, 1929), 212–234.

5. Kurt Bergengren, *När skönheten kom till city* (Stockholm: Aldus, 1976), 225.

6. Ibid., 226.

7. Lewerentz had collaborated with Asplund on the original layout of the cemetery and had designed the Chapel of the Resurrection. In 1930, the board of the cemetery decided to commission Asplund alone with the design of the crematorium and its chapel, dismissing Lewerentz. Claes Caldenby suggests that this decision was taken because of the 'board's dissatisfaction with Lewerentz's slow pace of work that was caused by his perfectionism'. Eva Eriksson, 'Rationalism and Classicism', in: Claes Caldenby, Jöran Lindvall and Wilfried Wang (eds.) *Sweden — Twentieth-Century Architecture* (Munich/New York: Prestel, 1998), 75.

8   Jan Henriksson, 'Arbetet på kontoret', in: Henrik O. Andersson et al. (eds.), *Peter Celsing — en bok om en arkitekt och hans verk* (Stockholm: Liber, 1980), 98.
9   Peter Celsing, 'Om Rummet', in: Henrik O. Andersson et al. (eds.), *Peter Celsing — en bok om en arkitekt och hans verk* (Stockholm: Liber, 1980), 118.
10 Celsing, 'Om Rummet', 119.
11 Ibid., 121.
12 Ibid., 121.
13 Ibid., 119.
14 Ibid., 120.
15 Ibid., 123.
16 Peter Celsing, 'Om Betongen', re-printed in: Marja-Riita Norri and Maija Kärkkainen (eds.) *Fasaden är mötet mellan ute och inne/The Façade is the Meeting between Outside and Inside* (Helsinki: Suomen rakennustaiteen museo/Finlands arkitekturmuseum, 1992), 52.
17 Celsing, 'Om Betongen', 52.
18 Ibid., 52.
19 Siegfried Giedion, *The Eternal Present — A Contribution on Constancy and Change* (London: Oxford University Press, 1962/63).
20 Henriksson, 'Arbetet på kontoret', 97.
21 Ibid., 99.
22 Ibid., 97.
23 Söve Olsson, testimony in Henrik O. Andersson et al. (eds.), *Peter Celsing — en bok om en arkitekt och hans verk* (Stockholm: Liber, 1980), 110.
24 Sivert Lindblom, testimony in Henrik O. Andersson et al. (eds.), *Peter Celsing — en bok om en arkitekt och hans verk* (Stockholm: Liber, 1980), 109.
25 By the time the idea of the stainless-steel façade was introduced, the theatre had already been rededicated for the temporary parliament. Henriksson 'Arbetet på kontoret', 99.
26 Henriksson 'Arbetet på kontoret', 97.
27 Ibid., 98.
28 Ibid., 98.

Bibliography

Andersson, Henrik O., 'Peter Celsing — från tunnelbana till kulturhus', in: Beate Sydhoff et al. (eds.), *1930/80 — Arkitektur, Form, Konst*, exhibition catalogue (Stockholm: Kulturhuset, 1980), 76–81

Bergengren, Kurt, *När skönheten kom till city* (Stockholm: Aldus, 1976)

Boëthius, Bertil (ed.), *Svenskt Biografiskt Lexikon*, vol. 18 (Stockholm: Albert Bonnier, 1929)

Caldenby, Claes, 'The Time of the Large Programmes 1960–75', in: Claes Caldenby, Jöran Lindvall and Wilfried Wang (eds.) *Sweden — Twentieth-Century Architecture* (Munich/New York: Prestel, 1998), 142–170

Celsing, Peter, 'Om Rummet', in: Henrik O. Andersson et al. (eds.), *Peter Celsing — En Bok om en Arkitekt och hans Verk* (Stockholm: Liber, 1980), 118–124

Celsing, Peter, 'Om Betongen', re-printed in: Marja-Riita Norri and Maija Kärkkainen (eds.), *Fasaden är mötet mellan ute och inne/The Façade is the Meeting between Outside and Inside* (Helsinki: Suomen rakennustaiteen museo/Finlands arkitekturmuseum, 1992), 45–52

Eriksson, Eva, 'Rationalism and Classicism', in: Claes Caldenby, Jöran Lindvall and Wilfried Wang (eds.) *Sweden — Twentieth-Century Architecture* (Munich/New York: Prestel, 1998), 46–79

Siegfried Giedion, *The Eternal Present — A Contribution on Constancy and Change* (London: Oxford University Press, 1962/63)

Henriksson, Jan, 'Arbetet på kontoret', in: Henrik O. Andersson et al. (eds.), *Peter Celsing — En Bok om en Arkitekt och hans Verk*, (Stockholm: Liber, 1980), 97–106

Material Knowledge and Cultural Values

Lara Schrijver

Polanyi's main proposition of tacit knowing is clearly articulated in his simple statement 'we can know more than we can tell'. It appeals to the intuitive understanding that there are aspects to what we do that are not at the surface but that do constitute a kind of 'knowing' that informs what we do. Polanyi's focus on the role of personal knowledge in tacit knowing has also revealed the fundamentally *situated* nature of knowledge. Polanyi argued that the aim of modern science in constructing an objective knowledge, detached from context and particulars, not only overlooks crucial aspects of knowledge but is in fact destructive of it.[1] His work has given rise to various investigations into how knowledge is constructed through both objective and quantifiable rules and tenets, and unstated habits or assumptions.[2] Throughout, most of these investigations are fundamentally anthropocentric, which should perhaps not be surprising, given that Polanyi himself focuses primarily on the role of the (individual) human mind in the process of knowledge acquisition, noting that the mind is more real than a cobblestone.[3] Nevertheless, in this article, I argue that his work opens the way for a more fundamental integration of matter and things into an understanding of tacit knowing, expanding the notion of the tacit from human agency in knowledge construction to an actor-network type of knowing. This is already made possible through the manner in which Polanyi articulates tacit knowing but becomes more plausible in the context of the 'new materialisms' that pay close attention to the independent role of things alongside human actors, suggesting that matter has its own agency.[4]

Polanyi's ideas on the tacit suggest that as much as we can codify some knowledge in rules and general tenets, there are important insights that are accessible but not necessarily explicated. In part, this has to do with what he identifies as a key feature of tacit knowing: the integration of subsidiary particulars within a coherent whole.[5] Physical skills provide a relatively self-evident example; in learning to sketch a building plan in pencil, there are aspects involved such as drawing a straight line, approximating horizontal and vertical proportions, and pressure on the pencil in order to modify line weight or thickness. These aspects are not *themselves* at stake; they are integrated into the focal knowing of how the plan should be drawn. Polanyi addresses this in relation to understanding and recognizing faces: the separate features are not themselves in focus but rather stand in the function of recognizing the face as a whole.[6] This type of knowing requires more than explication and codification: it requires a certain knowledge of context and undertones. The unstated and uncodified elements of knowledge are in that sense subsidiary parts of a skill (or of understanding a network of features), which rarely come into focus but are crucial to its workings.

As noted above, many studies have focused primarily on the human agency in tacit knowing, informed by, on the one hand, individual knowledge, and on the other hand, its social context. Tacit knowledge is then explored as an eminently social process, typically founded upon the transfer of knowledge by example and through experience.[7] In architecture, for example, this focus on the role and agency of human actors can be studied in studio exchanges, where the interaction between teacher and student is informed by more than just explicit requirements such as programme. This might equally include the modalities of personal knowledge and experience (the studio master) as well as the general cultural *habitus* of the studio and the discipline.[8] Yet alongside the tacit knowing residing in the designer or the design team, there are also material elements involved in this exchange. In architecture, this might materialize in the sketches or notes of a design meeting, or in the models used at different stages of the design process, all of which have remained slightly out of focus in this discussion. Notwithstanding an increasing interest in material objects and their agency in the world, the philosophical tracts on object ontologies remain somewhat abstracted, and conversely, architecture debates examine their objects closely but do not always attempt to draw more general insights from these particular cases.

Moreover, with discourse shifting away from 'objective' truths since roughly the 1970s, a number of interesting theoretical positions have paved the way for a more thorough evaluation of the role of material objects in these disciplines. Post-structuralist theory, science and technology studies, and actor-network theory are beginning to provide a vocabulary for rethinking human agency and develop a more embedded discourse that regrounds human actants in perpetual relation to their material counterparts.[9] As such, the rise in new materialisms and ideas such as 'vibrant matter' and material agency may help to include 'things' in explorations of tacit knowing.[10] This would allow investigations into tacit knowledge to not only focus on the informal and unstated habits and conventions in social interaction – all tied to human perception and agency – but also to include the agency of objects. Building on the ideas of actor-network theory and contemporary new materialisms, this approach then extends the anthropocentric core of tacit knowing to include the non-human.

Historical underpinnings: anthropocentric materialisms and cultural values

To bring these issues into focus, it is worth taking a brief detour through two earlier thinkers, John Ruskin and Siegfried Kracauer, who explicitly address material articulations in relation to cultural values and intentions. In his reflections on (and concerns about) industrialization in building, Ruskin directly focuses on material and craftsmanship, both as an expression of vitality. In *Seven Lamps*, Ruskin in some fashion situates the architectural project itself as a translator between making and understanding, suggesting that an observer or user can directly apprehend 'that some places have been delighted in more than others – that there has been a pause, and a care about them; and then there will come careless bits, and fast bits'.[11] As such, he suggests a certain type of implicit legibility – the kind that will allow a transfer of sensibility between craftsman and user by virtue of a hidden and further undisclosed mechanism.[12] While Ruskin does not explain how this transfer might come about, simply noting that it can be immediately 'seen', it does articulate his difficulty with envisioning empathy and connection to things in the industrial age.[13] Like many of his contemporaries, Ruskin was thinking through the consequences for buildings of industrial production. His turn to the craftsman suggests that minor flaws, imperfections and expressions of individuality signal vitality.

Another notable example of the values implicated in (artistic) production is the work of Siegfried Kracauer, which has received increasing attention in architecture theory since the 1995 translation of his Weimar essays into English.[14] Together with Walter Benjamin, he was one of the first to address the products of mass culture as a diagnostic tool – a form of seismograph – for the rumblings underneath the explicit societal values of a particular time. His work remains relevant today, particularly as it addresses the articulation of intentions and values in the cultural expressions of a society and its time. To Kracauer, this extends to both the explicit aims and wishes of a society, and its more hidden habits and values.[15] In this sense, his work already provides a foundation for more synthetic explorations of value today, as it addresses more than simply isolated aspects or explicit propositions. His Weimar essays critically reflect on a variety of cultural expressions (Berlin cinemas, Hollywood films, hotel lobbies) in which he sees a more general cultural *habitus*. As such, he provides some grounds for the supposition that the architectural object itself (the building, the drawing, the urban plan) incorporates a tacit expression of values, which is thereby correlated to its explicit intentions.

Bringing this idea of cultural values into the present, it becomes important to realize that matter itself has an autonomous existence alongside the projected values. While Kracauer already articulates negotiation between explicit positions, tacit values and matter, current ideas on the agency of things recalibrate his work, setting matter more clearly at the core of understanding the relationship between cultural expressions and underlying values. This requires taking into account the alignment of intentions and values while simultaneously acknowledging that these two aspects are *weakly aligned*. There are correlations, tangible and sometimes even legible, but the bond between values and intention within the matter is situated in time and place; this bond can be severed and reconstructed, infused with new values and cultural stories. This is perhaps the most important correction to modernist thinking in architecture, which built on a simplified version of Ruskin's transfer of sensibilities to assume a self-evident and often causal relation between artistic intention and material articulation.

It is this weak alignment between intentions and matter that has remained somehow out of sight and that has the ability to bring the negotiation between knowing *that* and knowing *how* into clear focus.[16] Any form of alignment between what the artist intends and the observer perceives is based on a constellation of knowledge, perception and assumptions, and includes a broad spectrum of both implicit and explicit elements of knowledge. It is, moreover, *situated in matter*, which is itself an independent actant. In this sense, the early insights of Polanyi and Ryle aid in differentiating aspects of human agency (in terms of experience-based and embodied knowledge) and material agency (in terms of its presence in knowing *how*). At the same time, the history of architecture thinking also provides valuable touchstones, which speak of the manner in which a building, an ornament or a drawing can contain dimensions of knowledge and understanding. Particularly in the context of new and emerging ecological sensibilities, the very idea that matter can independently connect with its observer, appealing to an intention to treat it with care, for example, suggests the potential to renew the general understanding of architecture as something that matters.

From human agency to actor-networks

The current shift to thinking through actor-networks and vibrant matter provides an additional perspective to the idea of a cultural diagnostic. In this perspective, the appeal to re-examine the values within things becomes about so much more – thinkers such as Timothy Morton and Jane Bennett reveal the unforeseen effects of matter, addressing things as autonomous entities that reconfigure the idea of human agency as it has been conceived throughout the twentieth century – they show how matter pushes back. Uncomfortable as this may be in resettling the boundaries between human and non-human actors, it is to some degree liberating and also familiar within architecture. It suggests that our things can have a life far beyond what we inject into them. It is here – in the complicated confluence of vibrant matter, human sensibility and contextual relationality – that more is to be explored.

One of the first moments that this deep interconnection between human agents and their material surroundings was approached as a new theoretical perspective was with the emergence of actor-network theory (ANT) in the mid-1980s.[17] The notion of care and concern was clearly articulated by Bruno Latour in 2004 when he closely analysed the mechanisms of criticism and suggested that for critics, the thing that is assembled should be treated with care.[18] Here, he brings the variety of associations that contribute to an object and its relationships, in order to show the beauty and simultaneously fragility of these constructions. Yet one might equally suggest that the things themselves are quite robust – Yaneva's analysis of the OMA models shows something like this, when she traces the life of models within the office, including their recuperation for other projects.[19] And this particular tracing shows hints of a weakly defined intentionality – the model of a project that has been fully articulated in relation to a particular question and programme, for example, can be recuperated as a model, understood at a different scale and then reworked in a fully different way.

These complicated and often problematic correlations may lead to the conclusion that there is no inherent value-based dimension in architecture.[20] However, the very desire to build an alternate environment almost by necessity contains a belief in 'the good' *embedded* within the very material of the envisioned project. It is, however, precisely because the values are situational and weakly aligned with the material that they represent a continuing negotiation between context and intention. Some values and contextual dimensions may (appear to) be materialized, and these can be examined in relation to cultural values and ideas about their material articulation.

There are some issues that may be useful to separate, however. The extended agency of ANT and new materialisms might be applied in a more limited fashion. Materials cannot themselves be said to have an ethical agency in the traditional sense, as brick and glass have no consciousness. At the same time, the idea of a weakly defined correlation between intentionality and effects can help explore the agency and knowledge of material objects. For this, it may be more helpful to turn to the implicit ethical appeal that resides in perception and is more contextually dependent. Building is thus not a *conscious* agent but becomes a *cultural* agent in the sense of Kracauer: it is present, it can be used, it is perceived and discussed, and as such it not only engages with but also expresses the undercurrents of society.

In search of a material consciousness

While the material dimension, as something that lacks conscious will or intent, may not have the same type of effects as human agents, the modern focus on universal tenets has negated the unforeseen effects of matter that is not delimited by human intentionality. Actor-network theory and new materialisms are, at heart, deeply relational. They examine things in light of both their autonomy and their situatedness. As such, they introduce an openness in the object, which can be subsequently re-coded and re-energized with new cultural codes. More importantly, they present an independence of matter, which reconfigures the typically instrumental relationships that modern science and architecture have assumed: that matter is simply a tool to be manipulated. ANT addresses the contextuality of the network (which includes non-human agents) and adds the material object as an agent of equal standing to humans. This combination of the autonomy of material objects and the relationality of the network can aid in addressing the particularities of architectural examples. It allows for an examination of the life of things and their effects, of observers and of surroundings, and potentially their role in creating a general *habitus*.

Might it thus be possible to envision some kind of ethical dimension that aligns with these new materialist approaches? This would suggest a mode of object-based reflection that allows for both the autonomy of the materialist understanding and the cultural values that are more relationally defined. This synthesis would require an awareness of the multiple appeals within the object, which both provide individual distinction on the basis of material properties and yet work in an integrated manner, appealing to more generally held cultural values. Additionally, it would require a permanent awareness of the incongruent relationship between intent and reception. The primary failure of political art is in its single-minded presumption of the reception of its 'message'. While an embedded political or moral appeal may be conceived of as such by the observer of the artwork or work of architecture, there is always the possibility that it will be overlooked or misunderstood. At the same time, the history of architecture provides examples of attributes that suggest particular values. Fragility may not demand care, but it does suggest it. As such, I would like to argue for revisiting material architectural qualities, which can be described and experienced, for their implicit promises – their desire, as it were, for a world more perfect than the one we inhabit.

One final important condition to address is that of *material resistance*.[21] This positions the architectural object and its subsidiary components (design, drawings, models, realized building) as a material manifestation that engages with the individual observer and cultural network as a whole. As such, it moves beyond universalist ideas of architecture as a cultural expression that provides a blueprint of societal codes and intentions. Instead, material resistance signals the autonomy of things. It shows that matter is not only shaped by human intentionality but also possesses its own qualities, and more importantly, that it pushes back.

On a cultural level, particularly in this age of faith in the endless agency of humankind and technology, this may also include literal material resistance such as the limitations presented by the material used. These limitations then become instrumental in reformulating the sense of endless possibility, suggesting a level of humility. Necessary to this is an enhanced sensitivity to the implications of a material object – both on the level of immediate apprehension, in what is directly legible, and on the level of underlying suppositions, cultural codes and conditions of production. The vocabulary of architecture until now has offered many handholds for metaphorical expressions of values and ethical dimensions but relatively little correlated to the material object. More attention on the dimension may help us forward. This will immediately lead to more complexity – as the question of a 'sustainable building', for example, then encompasses much more than the immediate material impact or technological implications. It may include the spatial organization that enables various forms of reuse – not by technological flexibility but rather sufficient space; it may be the kind of building that becomes a cultural emblem such that it remains valued enough to be reused; it may be the kind of building that builds upon its predecessors, or in contrast, something that presents a radical alternative. In all of these instances, however, the assessment is untenable if based only on a quantitative listing of costs and benefits; it requires a qualitative discussion, including contextualist arguments that explicate the implicit suppositions with which the building is imbued.

The very notion of material resistance incorporates an appreciation of particularity, as each action (intellectual or physical) induces an encounter with the response of the thing – this specific thing – which may lead to general principles but is not in itself a general thing. At the same time, this approach does not, as some fear, eliminate the particularity of human agency and perception. The condition of judgement remains present, as a counterforce to technocratic ideas of optimization, to the possibility of scientifically identifying a 'best' practice within generally wicked problems. Questions of judgement go to the heart of what we hope to do and to be. In other words, if we take discernment and careful observation as the space to escape codification, as creating the room for the agency of matter as well, then perhaps this is where we can explicitly begin to define our value systems. This should stand in some kind of relation to rational discourse but will be reconfigured by its attention to matter.[22] It simply requires an acknowledgement that 'works of art have multiple dimensions of value, including not only aesthetic and moral values, but historical, sociological, political, anthropological and other sorts of values as well'.[23] It is these multiple dimensions that ANT brings into focus and that new materialisms enrich with a more thorough understanding of material things as autonomous entities.

The history of architecture has mainly focused on anthropocentric values and the agency of the architect (such as due diligence and professionalism), assuming, or building on, a naturalized connection between human conduct and the results of design. By contrast, a materialist-oriented perspective allows for unforeseen results and changing circumstances – precisely within the bandwidth of understanding some of its appeals and intentions to be tacit and, therefore, not 'unknown' but rather incorporating affordances by their very nature, and thus allowing for not only the unforeseen in reception and use but also for fundamental transformations and recuperation.[24] As is clear from the other articles in this book, this raises many questions both on the level of the design process (the perspective of the architect), the object (the material perspective) and the user (the relational perspective). In this sense, it encourages an approach of fostering relations, thereby situating ourselves back in the network of the world-as-it-is, as one of many agents, from wood wide webs to vibrant matter.[25]

Notes

1. Michael Polanyi, *The Tacit Dimension* (Chicago: University of Chicago Press, 1966/2009), 20.
2. For example, Bo Göranzon, Maria Hammarén and Richard Ennals (eds.), *Dialogue, Skill and Tacit Knowledge* (Chichester, England: J. Wiley & Sons, 2006); Stephen P. Turner, *The Social Theory of Practices: Tradition, Tacit Knowledge, and Presuppositions* (Chicago: University of Chicago Press, 1994).
3. He notes that 'minds and problems possess a deeper reality than cobblestones, although cobblestones are admittedly more real in the sense of being *tangible*'. Polanyi, *The Tacit Dimension*, 33.
4. Diana Coole and Samantha Frost (eds.), *New Materialisms: Ontology, Agency, and Politics* (Durham: Duke University Press, 2010).
5. Polanyi, *The Tacit Dimension*, 7–10.
6. Polanyi provides an additional reflection on this general ability through witness descriptions in police procedures, where the particular examples of individual features are in specific focus but again in relation to providing a general description. Polanyi, *The Tacit Dimension*, 4–5.
7. Stephen P. Turner, *Understanding the Tacit* (London: Routledge, 2014). This is also addressed by Richard Sennett in *The Craftsman* (London: Allen Lane, 2008), 53–80, where he discusses medieval apprenticeship and the Renaissance workshop.
8. Pierre Bourdieu, *Outline of a Theory of Practice*, R. Nice (transl.), (Cambridge: Cambridge University Press, 1977). Bourdieu's idea of *habitus* is related to the ideas of tacit knowing, particularly in its unarticulated but formative structuring mechanisms, which Bourdieu sees as collectively and unconsciously orchestrated. In architecture, this may become visible in particular schools.
9. See, for example, Michel Foucault, *The Order of Things: An Archaeology of the Human Sciences* (New York: Vintage Books, 1970 [orig. *Les mots et les choses*, 1966]); Isabelle Stengers, *In Catastrophic Times. Resisting the Coming Barbarism*, A. Goffey (transl.), (Open Humanities Press/Meson Press, 2015 [orig. *Au temps des catastrophes*, 2009]); John Law (ed.), *Power, Action, and Belief: A New Sociology of Knowledge?* (London/Boston: Routledge & Kegan Paul, 1986); Bruno Latour, *Reassembling the Social: An Introduction to Actor-Network-Theory* (Oxford: Oxford University Press, 2005).
10. See, for example, Jane Bennett, *Vibrant Matter: A Political Ecology of Things* (Durham: Duke University Press, 2010); Timothy Morton, *Dark Ecology. For a Logic of Future Coexistence* (New York: Columbia University Press, 2016); Coole and Frost (eds.), *New Materialisms*.
11. These are introductory lines in Section XXI of the Lamp of Life, where he further observes that 'sculpture is not the mere cutting of the form of anything in stone; it is the cutting of the effect of it'. John Ruskin, *The Seven Lamps of Architecture* (London: Smith, Elder & Co., 1849), 141–142 (par. XXI).
12. Ruskin largely limits this to only the transfer of a sensibility, while modernist architecture expands this to a perceived correlation between intention and reception. Yet here, I follow Polanyi's concern that generally held tenets are problematic. Each work of design or material object is defined less by a metaphysical and inherent quality as it is a suggestion and framework informed by currently held values, which may be subsequently transformed or reconstituted.
13. John Ruskin, *The Seven Lamps of Architecture* (London: Smith, Elder & Co., 1849).
14. Siegfried Kracauer, *The Mass Ornament: Weimar Essays*, Thomas Levin (transl.), (Cambridge, MA: Harvard University Press, 1995 [orig. *Das Ornament der Masse*, 1963]).
15. Siegfried Kracauer, 'The Mass Ornament', in Kracauer, *The Mass Ornament: Weimar Essays*, 75–86.

16   This is especially with attention to the particularities of knowing *how*, which does not require theoretical understanding but does require a grasp of principles and the ability to act in accordance with the desired results. Gilbert Ryle, 'Knowing How and Knowing That: The Presidential Address', *Proceedings of the Aristotelian Society*, 46:1 (1946), 1–16.

17   The book usually credited as the starting point of ANT is John Law (ed.), *Power, Action, and Belief*.

18   Bruno Latour, 'Why Has Critique Run out of Steam? From Matters of Fact to Matters of Concern', *Critical Inquiry* 30 (Winter 2004), 225–248.

19   Albena Yaneva, *Made by the Office for Metropolitan Architecture: An Ethnography of Design* (Rotterdam: nai010 Publishers, 2009).

20   This seems to underlie many of the positions in the 1970s and 1980s, in which formal concerns were emphasized as a distanciation from sociopolitical and ethical concerns.

21   Richard Sennett, *The Craftsman* (London: Allen Lane, 2008).

22   See, for example, Greet De Block and Vera Vicenzotti, 'The Effects of Affect. A Plea for Distance Between the Human and Non-human', *JoLA: Journal of Landscape Architecture* 13:2 (2018), 46–55.

23   Jeffrey Dean, 'Ethics and Aesthetics: The State of the Art', *Aesthetics Online*, 2002, American Society for Aesthetics. (online at: aesthetics-online.org/general/custom.asp?page=DeanState. Last accessed December 18, 2020).

24   See James J. Gibson, *The Ecological Approach to Visual Perception* (Boston: Houghton Mifflin, 1979); and James J. Gibson, 'The Theory of Affordances', in: Robert Shaw and John Bransford (eds.), *Perceiving, Acting and Knowing: Toward an Ecological Psychology* (Hillsdale, NJ: Lawrence Erlbaum, 1977), 67–82.

25   The 'wood wide web' refers to an underground mycorrhizal network that connects trees. The phrase was popularized by Suzanne Simard, one of the first to research these networks. Suzanne Simard, 'How Trees Talk to Each Other', TedSummit, June 2016, online at: www.ted.com/talks/suzanne_simard_how_trees_talk_to_each_other (last accessed January 4, 2021); see also Merlin Sheldrake, *Entangled Life. How Fungi Make Our Worlds, Change Our Minds, and Shape Our Futures* (London: The Bodley Head, 2020), 3–15, 165–193.

Bibliography

Bennett, Jane, *Vibrant Matter: A Political Ecology of Things* (Durham: Duke University Press, 2010)

Bourdieu, Pierre, *Outline of a Theory of Practice*, R. Nice (transl.), (Cambridge: Cambridge University Press, 1977)

Coole, Diana and Samantha Frost (eds.), *New Materialisms: Ontology, Agency, and Politics* (Durham: Duke University Press, 2010)

Dean, Jeffrey 'Ethics and Aesthetics: The State of the Art', *Aesthetics Online*, 2002, American Society for Aesthetics (online at: https://aesthetics-online.org/general/custom.asp?page=DeanState. Last accessed December 18, 2020)

De Block, Greet and Vera Vicenzotti, 'The Effects of Affect. A Plea for Distance Between the Human and Non-human', *JoLA: Journal of Landscape Architecture* 13:2 (2018), 46–55

Foucault, Michel, *The Order of Things: An Archaeology of the Human Sciences* (New York: Vintage Books, 1970 [orig. *Les Mots et les Choses*, 1966])

Gibson, James J., 'The Theory of Affordances', in: Robert Shaw and John Bransford (eds.), *Perceiving, Acting and Knowing: Toward an Ecological Psychology* (Hillsdale, NJ: Lawrence Erlbaum, 1977), 67–82

Gibson, James J., *The Ecological Approach to Visual Perception* (Boston: Houghton Mifflin, 1979)

Göranzon, Bo, Maria Hammarén and Richard Ennals (eds.), *Dialogue, Skill and Tacit Knowledge* (Chichester, England: J. Wiley & Sons, 2006)

Kracauer, Siegfried, *The Mass Ornament: Weimar Essays*, Thomas Levin (transl.), (Cambridge, MA: Harvard University Press, 1995 [orig. *Das Ornament der Masse*, 1963])

Latour, Bruno, 'Why Has Critique Run out of Steam? From Matters of Fact to Matters of Concern', *Critical Inquiry* 30 (Winter 2004), 225–248

Latour, Bruno, *Reassembling the Social: An Introduction to Actor-Network-Theory* (Oxford: Oxford University Press, 2005)

Law, John (ed.), *Power, Action, and Belief: A New Sociology of Knowledge?* (London/Boston: Routledge & Kegan Paul, 1986)

Morton, Timothy, *Dark Ecology. For a Logic of Future Coexistence* (New York: Columbia University Press, 2016)

Polanyi, Michael, *The Tacit Dimension* (Chicago: University of Chicago Press, 1966/2009)

Ruskin, John, *The Seven Lamps of Architecture* (London: Smith, Elder & Co., 1849)

Ryle, Gilbert, 'Knowing How and Knowing That: The Presidential Address', *Proceedings of the Aristotelian Society*, New Series, 46:1 (1946), 1–16

Sennett, Richard, *The Craftsman* (London: Allen Lane, 2008)

Sheldrake, Merlin, *Entangled Life. How Fungi Make Our Worlds, Change Our Minds, and Shape Our Futures* (London: The Bodley Head, 2020)

Simard, Suzanne, 'How Trees Talk to Each Other', TedSummit, June 2016, www.ted.com/talks/suzanne_simard_how_trees_talk_to_each_other (last accessed January 4, 2021)

Stengers, Isabelle, *In Catastrophic Times. Resisting the Coming Barbarism*, A. Goffey (transl.), (Open Humanities Press/Meson Press, 2015 [orig. *Au Temps des Catastrophes*, 2009])

Turner, Stephen P., *The Social Theory of Practices: Tradition, Tacit Knowledge, and Presuppositions* (Chicago: University of Chicago Press, 1994)

Turner, Stephen P., *Understanding the Tacit* (London: Routledge, 2014)

Yaneva, Albena, *Made by the Office for Metropolitan Architecture: An Ethnography of Design* (Rotterdam: nai010 Publishers, 2009)

About the Authors

Tom Avermaete is a professor at ETH Zürich, where he is Chair for the History and Theory of Urban Design. Avermaete has a special research interest in the post-war public realm and the architecture of the city in Western and non-Western contexts. He is the author of *Another Modern: The Post-War Architecture and Urbanism of Candilis-Josic-Woods* (2005) and *Casablanca, Chandigarh: A Report on Modernization* (2014, with Casciato). Avermaete has also edited numerous books, including *Shopping Towns Europe* (with Gosseye, 2017), *Acculturating the Shopping Centre* (with Gosseye, 2018) and *The New Urban Condition* (with Medrano and Recaman, 2021). He is a member of the editorial team of *OASE Architectural Journal* and the advisory board of the *Architectural Theory Review*, among others.

Margitta Buchert is the Chair for Architecture and Art 20th/21st Centuries at the Leibniz University of Hanover Faculty of Architecture and Landscape Sciences. Her focus is on architectural theory, design theory and design principles, and her primary fields of research are reflexive design and urban architecture, as well as the aesthetics and contextuality of architecture, art, cities and nature. Her publications include *Shaping Design. Media of Architectural Conception* (2020); 'Bigness and Porosity' in Sophie Wolfrum et al., *Porous City* (2018); *Processes of Reflexive Design* (2018); 'Mobile und Stabile' in Anett Zinsmeister, *Figure of Motion* (2011); and 'Actuating. Koolhaas' Urban Aesthetics' in Jale Erzen, *Mirmarlikta Estetik Dusunce* (2010).

Christoph Grafe is Professor of Architectural History and Theory at the University of Wuppertal and Vice Dean of Research of the Faculty of Architecture and Building Engineering. He was Director of the Flanders Architecture Institute in Antwerp (2011-2017) and visiting professor at the Politecnico di Milano and the University of Hasselt (Belgium). He is the author of *People's Palaces* (2014) and *Umbaukultur:*

The Architecture of Altering (2020, with Tim Rieniets). He is the editor of *OASE* and *Eselsohren* and was a member of the editorial board of the *Journal of Architecture* from 2007 to 2020. He is on the advisory board of the Baukunstarchiv Nordrhein-Westfalen and the board of directors at z33 in Hasselt (Belgium). In 2015, he served as interim city architect in Antwerp together with Bob Van Reeth.

Mari Lending is a professor in architectural theory and history at the Oslo School of Architecture and Design and a founding member of the Oslo Centre for Critical Architectural Studies (OCCAS). She is currently Vice President of the European Architectural History Network. She is the author of *Plaster Monuments. Architecture and the Power of Reproduction* (2017), *A Feeling of History* (2018, with Peter Zumthor), and *Images of Egypt* (2018, with Eirik Bøhn and Tim Anstey). Her latest book is, with Erik Langdalen, *Sverre Fehn, Nordic Pavilion, Venice. Voices from the Archives* (2021).

Angelika Schnell is Professor for Architectural Theory, Architectural History and Design at the Academy of Fine Arts Vienna. She is the former editor of *ARCH+*, current member of the editorial boards of *ARCH+* and *Candide*, and co-editor of *Bauwelt Fundamente*. She has numerous publications and lectures at international institutions. Her dissertation (summa cum laude) was on the theoretical work of Aldo Rossi. Her research foci are on the relationship between architecture and urbanism in the twentieth and twenty-first centuries, in particular on the criticism of modernism and its historiographical conception, design methods and their transdisciplinary interconnections.

Eireen Schreurs is a founding partner of SUBoffice architects, which combines a building practice with an architectural research portfolio. She teaches at Delft University of Technology and Sint-Lucas in Ghent. As a PhD fellow at the KU Leuven/University of Antwerp she is currently preparing her dissertation on material culture, or how materials acquire meaning in architecture. She was co-editor of *The New Craft School* (2018) as well as a member of the editorial board of the *Flanders Architectural Review* (2020). In her work as a designer, researcher and teacher, her interest lies in 'the existing' in the broadest sense – culturally, socially and materially – and how this can instigate new forms of architecture.

Lara Schrijver is Professor in Architecture Theory at the University of Antwerp Faculty of Design Sciences. She has previously taught at Delft University of Technology (2005-2014) and the Rotterdam Academy of Architecture (2007-2013). She is the editor for the *KNOB Bulletin* and *SPOOL*, and has served as editor for *Footprint* journal and *OASE*. Her work has been published in various academic and professional journals. She is the author of *Radical Games* (2009) and co-editor of *Autonomous Architecture in Flanders* (2016). She was also co-editor for three editions of the annual review *Architecture in the Netherlands* (2016-2019).

www.ingramcontent.com/pod-product-compliance
Ingram Content Group UK Ltd.
Pitfield, Milton Keynes, MK11 3LW, UK
UKHW021842140426
5217IPUK00022B/1548